HAPPY POLLYOOLY

The Rich Little Poor Girl

EDGAR JEPSON

1st WORLD LIBRARY
Literary Society

Happy Pollyooly

Edgar Jepson

© 1st World Library, 2007
PO Box 2211
Fairfield, IA 52556
www.1stworldlibrary.com
First Edition

LCCN: 2007930730

Softcover ISBN: 978-1-4218-4811-2
Hardcover ISBN: 978-1-4218-4714-6
eBook ISBN: 978-1-4218-4908-9

Purchase *"Happy Pollyooly"*
as a traditional bound book at:
www.1stWorldLibrary.com/purchase.asp?ISBN=978-1-4218-4811-2

1st World Library is a literary, educational organization
dedicated to:

- Creating a free internet library of downloadable ebooks

- Hosting writing competitions and offering book publishing
  scholarships.

Interested in more 1st World Library books? contact:
literacy@1stworldlibrary.com
Check us out at: www.1stworldlibrary.com

1ˢᵗ World Library Literary Society

Giving Back to the World

"If you want to work on the core problem, it's early school literacy."

- James Barksdale, former CEO of Netscape

"No skill is more crucial to the future of a child, or to a democratic and prosperous society, than literacy."

- Los Angeles Times

"Literacy... means far more than learning how to read and write... The aim is to transmit... knowledge and promote social participation."

- UNESCO

"Literacy is not a luxury, it is a right and a responsibility. If our world is to meet the challenges of the twenty-first century we must harness the energy and creativity of all our citizens."

- President Bill Clinton

"Parents should be encouraged to read to their children, and teachers should be equipped with all available techniques for teaching literacy, so the varying needs and capacities of individual kids can be taken into account."

- Hugh Mackay

CONTENTS

CHAPTER I

THE HONOURABLE JOHN RUFFIN
MAKES AN ARRANGEMENT

The angel child looked at the letter from Buda-Pesth with lively interest, for she knew that it came from her friend and patroness Esmeralda, the dancer, who was engaged in a triumphant tour of the continent of Europe. She put it on the top of the pile of letters, mostly bills, which had come for her employer, the Honourable John Ruffin, set the pile beside his plate, and returned to the preparation of his breakfast.

She looked full young to hold the post of house-keeper to a barrister of the Inner Temple, for she was not yet thirteen; but there was an uncommonly capable intentness in her deep blue eyes as she watched the bacon, sizzling on the grill, for the right moment to turn the rashers. She never missed it. Now and again those deep blue eyes sparkled at the thought that the Honourable John Ruffin would presently give her news of her brilliant friend.

She heard him come out of his bedroom, and at once dished up his bacon, and carried it into his sitting-room. She found him already reading the letter, and saw that it was giving him no pleasure. His lips were set in a thin line; there was a frown on his brow and an angry gleam in his grey eyes. She knew that of all the emotions which moved him, anger was the rarest; indeed she could only remember having once seen him angry: on the occasion on which he had smitten Mr. Montague Fitzgerald on the head when that shining money-lender was trying to force from her the key of his chambers; and she wondered what had been happening to the Esmeralda to annoy him. She was too loyal to suppose that anything that the Esmeralda had herself done could be annoying him.

He ate his breakfast more slowly than usual, and with a brooding air. His eyes never once, as was their custom, rested with warm appreciation on Pollyooly's beautiful face, set in its aureole of red hair; he did not enliven his meal by talking to her about the affairs of the moment. She respected his musing, and waited on him in silence. She had cleared away the breakfast tray and was folding the table-cloth when, at last, he broke his thoughtful silence.

"There's nothing for it: I must go to Buda-Pesth," he said with a resolute air.

"There's nothing the matter with the Esmeralda, sir?" said Pollyooly with quick anxiety.

"There's something very much the matter with the Esmeralda—a Moldo-Wallachian," said the Honourable John Ruffin with stern coldness.

"Is it an illness, sir?" said Pollyooly yet more anxiously.

"No; it's a nobleman," said the Honourable John Ruffin with even colder sternness.

Pollyooly pondered the matter for a few seconds; then she said: "Is he—is he persecuting her, sir, like Senor Perez did

Edgar Jepson

when I was dancing with her in 'Titania's Awakening'?"

"It ought to be a persecution; but I fear it isn't," said the Honourable John Ruffin grimly. "I gather from this letter that she is regarding his attentions, which, I am sure, consist chiefly of fulsome flattery and uncouth gifts, with positive approbation."

Pollyooly pondered this information also; then she said:

"Is she going to marry him, sir?"

"She is not!" said the Honourable John Ruffin in a tone of the deepest conviction but rather loudly.

Pollyooly looked at him and waited for further information to throw light on his manifest disturbance of spirit.

He drummed a tattoo on the bare table with his fingers, frowning the while; then he said:

"Constancy to the ideal, though perhaps out of place in a man, is alike woman's privilege and her duty. I should be sorry—indeed I should be deeply shocked if the Esmeralda were to fail in that duty."

"Yes, sir," said Pollyooly in polite sympathy, though she had not the slightest notion what he meant.

"Especially since I took such pains to present to her the true ideal—the English ideal," he went on. "Whereas this Moldo-Wallachian—at least that's what I gather from this letter—is merely handsome in that cheap and obvious South-European way—that is to say he has big, black eyes, probably liquid, and a large, probably flowing, moustache. Therefore I go to Buda-Pesth."

"Yes, sir," said Pollyooly with the same politeness and in the same ignorance of his reason for going.

"I shall wire to her to-day—to give her pause—and to-morrow I shall start." He paused, looking at her thoughtfully for a moment, then went on: "I should like to take you with me, for I know how helpful you can be in the matter of these insolent and infatuated foreigners. But Buda-Pesth is too far away. And the question is what I am going to do with you while I'm away."

"We can stay here all right, sir—the Lump and me," said Pollyooly quickly, with a note of surprise in her voice.

Her little brother, Roger, who lived with her in the airy attic above the Honourable John Ruffin's chambers, had acquired the name of "The Lump" from his admirable placidity.

"I don't like the idea of your doing that," he said, shaking his head and frowning. "I don't know how long I may be away—the affirmation of the ideal is sometimes a lengthy process. Of course the Temple is a quiet place; but I don't like to leave two small children alone in it for a fortnight, or three weeks. It isn't as if Mr. Gedge-Tomkins were at home. If he were at hand—just across the landing, it would be a very different matter."

"But I'm *sure* we should be all right, sir," said Pollyooly with entire confidence.

"Oh, I'm bound to say that if any child in the world could take care of herself and a little brother, it's you," he said handsomely. "But I want to devote all my energies to the affirmation of the ideal; and I must not be troubled by anxiety about you. I shall have to dispose of you safely somehow."

Edgar Jepson

With that he rose, lighted a cigar, and presently sallied forth into the world. The matter of learning the quickest way to Buda-Pesth and procuring a ticket for the morrow took him little more than half an hour. Then the matter of disposing safely of Pollyooly and the Lump during his absence rose again to his mind and he walked along pondering it. Presently there came to him a happy thought: there was their common friend, Hilary Vance, an artist who had employed Pollyooly as his model for a set of stories for *The Blue Magazine*. Hilary Vance was devoted to Pollyooly, and he had a spare bedroom. But for a while the Honourable John Ruffin hesitated; the artist was a man of an uncommonly mercurial, irresponsible temperament. Was it safe to entrust two small children to his care? Then he reflected that Pollyooly was a strong corrective of irresponsibility, and took a taxicab to Chelsea.

Hilary Vance, very broad, very thick, very round, with a fine, rebellious mop of tow-coloured hair, which had fallen forward so as nearly to hide his big, simple eyes, opened the door to him. At the sight of his visitor a spacious round smile spread over his spacious face; and he welcomed him with an effusive enthusiasm.

At his christening the good fairy had given to the Honourable John Ruffin a very lively interest in his fellow-creatures and a considerable power of observation with which to gratify it. He was used to the splendid expansiveness of Hilary Vance; but it seemed to him that to-day he was boiling with an added exuberance; and that curiosity was aroused. He took up a chair and hammered its back on the floor so that the dust fell off the seat, sat down astride it, and, bending forward a little, proceeded to observe the artist with very keen eyes. Hilary Vance, who was very busy, fell to work again, and after his manner, grew grandiloquent about the pleasures of the day before, which he had spent in the country.

Soon it grew clear to the Honourable John Ruffin that his friend had swollen with the insolent happiness so hateful to the Fates, and he said:

"You seem to be uncommonly cheerful, Vance. What's the matter?"

Hilary Vance looked at him gravely, drew himself upright in his chair, laid down his pencil, and said in a tone of solemnity calculated to awaken the deepest respect and awe:

"Ruffin, I have found a woman—a WOMAN!"

The quality of the Honourable John Ruffin's gaze changed; his eyes rested on the face of his friend with a caressing, almost cherishing, delight.

"Isn't it becoming rather a habit?" he said blandly.

"I don't know what you mean," said Hilary Vance with splendid dignity. "But this is different. This is a WOMAN!"

His face filled with an expression of the finest beatitude.

"They so often are," said the Honourable John Ruffin. "Does James know about her?"

At the sound of the name of the mentor and friend who had rescued him from so many difficulties, something of guilt mingled with the beatitude on Hilary Vance's face, and he said in a less assured tone:

"James is in Scotland."

The Honourable John Ruffin sprang from his chair with a briskness which made Hilary Vance himself jump, and cried in a tone of the liveliest commiseration and dismay:

"Good Heavens! Then you're lost—lost!"

"What do you mean?" said Hilary Vance quite sharply.

"I mean that your case is hopeless," said the Honourable John Ruffin in a less excited tone. "*James* is in Scotland; *I'm* off to Buda-Pesth; and *you* have found a WOMAN— probably THE WOMAN."

"I don't know what you mean," said Hilary Vance, frowning.

"That's the worst of it! That's why it's so hopeless!" said the Honourable John Ruffin in a tone of deep depression.

"What do you mean?" cried Hilary Vance in sudden bellow.

"Good-bye, old chap; good-bye," said the Honourable John Ruffin in the most mournful tone and with the most mournful air. "I *can not* save you. I've got to go to Buda-Pesth." He walked half-way to the door, turned sharply on his heel, clapped his hand to his head with the most dramatic gesture, and cried: "Stay! I'll wire to James!"

"I'm damned if you do!" bellowed Hilary Vance.

"I must! I must!" cried the Honourable John Ruffin, still dramatic.

"You don't know his address, thank goodness!" growled Hilary Vance triumphantly. "And you won't get it from me."

"I shan't? Then it's hopeless indeed," said the Honourable John Ruffin with a gesture of despair. He stood and seemed to plunge into deep reflection, while Hilary Vance scowled an immense scowl at him.

The Honourable John Ruffin allowed a faint air of hope to lighten his gloom; then he said:

"There's a chance—there's yet a chance!"

"I don't want any chance!" cried Hilary Vance stormily. "You can jolly well mind your own business and leave me alone. I can look after myself without any help from you—or James either."

"Whom the gods wish to destroy they first madden young," said the Honourable John Ruffin sadly. "But there's always Pollyooly; she may save you yet. I came to suggest that while I'm away in Buda-Pesth you should let Pollyooly and the Lump occupy that spare bedroom of yours. I don't like leaving them alone in the Temple; and I thought that you might like to have them here for a while, though I fear Pollyooly will clean the place." He looked round the studio gloomily. "But you can stand that for once, I expect," he went on more cheerfully. "At any rate it would be worth your while, because you'd learn what grilled bacon really is."

At the mention of the name of Pollyooly the scowl on Hilary Vance's face began to smooth out; as the Honourable John Ruffin developed his suggestion it slowly disappeared.

"Oh, yes; I'll put them up. I shall be delighted to," he said eagerly. "Pollyooly gives more delight to my eye than any one I know. And there are so few people in town, and I'm lonely at times. I wish I liked bacon, since she is so good at grilling it; but I don't."

The Honourable John Ruffin came several steps down the room wearing an air of the wildest amazement:

Edgar Jepson

"You don't like bacon?" he cried in astounded tones. "That explains everything. I've always wondered about you. Now I know. You are one of those whom the gods love; and I can't conceive why you didn't die younger."

"I don't know what you mean," said Hilary Vance, bristling and scowling again.

"You don't? Well, it doesn't matter. But I'm really very much obliged to you for relieving me of all anxiety about those children."

They discussed the hour at which Pollyooly and the Lump should come, and then the Honourable John Ruffin held out his hand.

But Hilary Vance rose and came to the front door with him. On the threshold he coughed gently and said:

"I should like you to see Flossie."

"Flossie?" said the Honourable John Ruffin. "Ah—the WOMAN." He looked at Hilary Vance very earnestly. "Yes, I see—I see—of course her name would be Flossie." Then he added sternly:

"No; if I saw her James might accuse me of having encouraged you. He would, in fact. He always does."

"She's only at the florist's just at the end of the street," said Hilary Vance in a persuasive tone.

"She would be," said the Honourable John Ruffin in a tone of extraordinary patience. "I don't know why it is that the WOMAN is so often at a florist's at the end of the street. It seems to be one of nature's strange whims." His face grew very gloomy again and in a very sad tone he added:

"Good-bye, poor old chap; good-bye!"

He shook hands firmly with his puzzled friend and started briskly up the street. Ten yards up it he paused, turned and called back:

"She's everything that's womanly, isn't she?"

"Yes—everything," cried Hilary Vance with fervour.

The Honourable John Ruffin shook his head sadly and without another word walked briskly on.

Hilary Vance, still looking puzzled, shut the door and went back to his studio. He failed, therefore, to perceive the Honourable John Ruffin enter the florist's shop at the end of the street. He did not come out of it for a quarter of an hour, and then he came out smiling. Seeing that he only brought with him a single rose, he had taken some time over its selection.

CHAPTER II

HILARY VANCE FINDS A CONFIDANTE

That afternoon, when Pollyooly was helping him pack his portmanteau for his journey to Buda-Pesth, the Honourable John Ruffin told her of the arrangement he had made with Hilary Vance, that she and the Lump should spend the time till his return at the studio at Chelsea.

Pollyooly's face brightened; and there was something of the joy which warriors feel in foemen worthy of their steel in the tone in which she said:

"Thank you, sir. I shall like that. It will be a change for the Lump; and I've always wanted to know what that studio would look like if once it were properly cleaned. That Mrs. Thomas who works for Mr. Vance does let it get so dirty."

"Yes; I told Mr. Vance that I was sure that you'd get the place really clean for him," said the Honourable John Ruffin with a chuckle.

"Oh, yes; I will," said Pollyooly firmly.

The Honourable John Ruffin chuckled again, and said:

"Mr. Vance is going to have the spring cleaning of a lifetime."

"Yes, sir. It's not quite summer-time yet," said Pollyooly.

The next morning before taking the train to Buda-Pesth, he despatched her, the Lump, and the brown tin box which contained their clothes, to Chelsea in a taxicab. Hilary Vance welcomed them with the most cordial exuberance, led the way to his spare bedroom, and with an entire unconsciousness of that bedroom's amazing resemblance to a long-forgotten dust-bin, invited Pollyooly to unpack the box and make herself at home.

Pollyooly gazed slowly round the room, and then she looked at her host in some discomfort. She was a well-mannered child, and careful of the feelings of a host. Then she said in a hesitating voice:

"I think I should like to—to—dust out the room before I unpack, please."

"By all means—by all means," said Hilary Vance cheerfully; and he went back to his work.

Owing to his absorption in it he failed to perceive the curious measures Pollyooly took to dust out the bedroom. She put on an apron, fastened up her hair and covered it with a large cotton handkerchief, rolled up her sleeves, and carried a broom, two pails of hot water from the kitchen, a scrubbing-brush, and a very large piece of soap into the room she proposed to dust. She shut herself in, took the counterpane off the bed, shook it with furious vigour, and even more vigourously still banged it against the end of the bedstead. When she had finished with it the counterpane was hardly white, but the room was dustier than ever. She covered up the bed again, took down the pictures and again made the room dustier. Then she swept the ceiling and the walls. After doing so she shook the counterpane again. And the room was still dusty; but the dust was nearly all on the floor, or on the black face of Pollyooly. She swept it up. Then she went quietly out into the street with the strips of carpet and banged them against the railings of the house; this time it was the street that was dustier than ever; and Pollyooly appeared to have come from the lower Congo. For the next half-hour, had he not been absorbed in his work, Hilary Vance might have heard a steady and sustained rasp of a scrubbing-brush.

Pollyooly came to the laying of the lunch with her angel face deeply flushed; but she wore a very cheerful air. Also she displayed an excellent appetite. In the middle of lunch she said in dreamy reminiscence, apropos of nothing in particular:

"I got this place clean once."

"Isn't it clean now?" said Hilary Vance in a tone of anxious surprise.

"It depends on what you call clean," said Pollyooly politely.

After lunch she brought the drawers from the chest of drawers in the bedroom into the kitchen and washed them and dried them in the sun. Then, at last, she unpacked the brown tin box and put away their clothes.

After that she took the Lump for an hour's walk on the embankment. She preferred it to the embankment below the Temple; it seemed to her airier. She returned to tea, and had a little struggle with the teaspoons. They enjoyed, after the lapse of months, the experience of shining. After tea Hilary Vance told her regretfully that he would not be able to come home to supper, but that she would find provisions in the cupboard, and advising them to go to bed early, bade them an affectionate good-night and went out in a northeasterly direction to talk about Art.

When the door closed behind him Pollyooly heaved a faint sigh of satisfaction and looked round the studio with the light of battle in her eye. Then she took the canvases, which were set against the wall three and four deep, into the street and brushed them. The dust in the street had been a tedious grey; in front of the house of Hilary Vance it became a warm black.

Then she put the Lump, with the toys she had brought with her, into the clean bedroom, and fell upon the studio. By the time she had brushed the pictures and the walls and the ceiling its floor had become very dusty indeed, and she was once more black. She swept it, and then she was an hour scrubbing it. When it was done she gave the Lump his supper and put him to bed. After supper she dealt faithfully with the windows. The skylight gave her trouble; it was so high. But she tied a wet cloth round the top of a broom, and by standing on the table reached it. It made her arms ache, but slowly the panes assumed a transparency to which they had long been unused. When she had cleaned them from the inside she considered thoughtfully the possibility of sitting astride the roof and cleaning their outside surfaces. But there was no way of getting on to the roof. Then she had a hot bath; she needed it.

Mrs. Thomas had been apprised of her coming and greeted her amiably. It is only fair to say that she gave the studio the cleaning it generally received without observing that anything whatever had happened to it.

Hilary Vance, who was of that rare, but happy, disposition,

came to breakfast in splendid spirits. He also did not observe that anything had happened to the studio. But when he got to his work he kept looking up from it with a puzzled air.

At last he said:

"It's odd—very odd. Lately I've been thinking that my sight was beginning to weaken. But this morning I can see quite clearly. Yet it isn't a very bright morning."

"Perhaps if you had the skylight cleaned on the outside, too, you'd see clearer still," said Pollyooly in the tone of one throwing out a careless suggestion.

Hilary Vance looked round the studio more earnestly:

"By Jove! You've cleaned it again!" he cried. "You are a brick, Pollyooly. But all the same you're my guest here; and it's not the function of a guest to clean her host's house. I ought to have remembered it and had it cleaned before you came."

"But I liked doing it. I did, really," said Pollyooly.

"You are undoubtedly a brick—a splendid brick," he said enthusiastically.

Hilary Vance was one of those great-hearted men of thirty who crave for sympathy; he must unbosom himself. Pollyooly was not quite the confidante of his ideal; but his mentor, James, the novelist (not Henry), was in Scotland; and the salt sea flowed between him and the Honourable John Ruffin. Pollyooly was at hand, and she was intelligent. No later than the next morning he began to talk to her of Flossie—her beauty, her charm, her sympathetic nature, her womanliness, and her intelligence.

Pollyooly received his confidences with the utmost politeness. She could not, indeed, follow him in his higher, finer flights; but she succeeded in keeping on her angel face an expression of sufficient appreciation to satisfy his unexacting mind. It is to be feared that she did not really appreciate the splendour of the passion he displayed before her; it is even to be feared that she regarded it as no more than a further eccentricity in an eccentric nature. She grew curious, however, to see the lady who had so enthralled him, and was, therefore, pleased when she suggested that she should relieve Mrs. Thomas of the housekeeping, that he accepted the suggestion and told her to procure, among other things, some flowers for the studio.

She found Flossie to be a fair, fluffy-haired, plump and pretty girl of twenty, entirely pleased with herself and the world. It seemed to Pollyooly that she gave herself airs. She came away with the flowers, finding the ecstasies of Mr. Hilary Vance as inexplicable as ever. But she did not puzzle over the matter at all, for it was none of her business; Mr. Vance was like that.

Having once begun, Hilary Vance fell into the way of confiding to her from day to day his hopes and fears, the varying fortunes of his suit. Some days the skies of his heaven were fair and serene; some days they were livid with the darkest kind of cloud. Pollyooly, by dint of hearing so much about it, began to get some understanding of the matter, and consequently to take a greater interest in it. Always she made an excellent listener. Her intercourse with the Honourable John Ruffin had taught her that a comprehension of the matter under discussion was by no means a necessary qualification of the excellent listener; and Hilary Vance grew entirely satisfied with his confidante.

The affair was pursuing the usual course of his affairs of the heart: one day he was well up in the seventh heaven, talking

Edgar Jepson

joyfully of an early proposal and an immediate marriage; another he was well down in the seventh hell. Pollyooly was always ready with the kind of sympathy, chiefly facial, the changing occasion demanded.

Then one day her host had gone out to lunch with an editor and she was taking hers with the Lump, when there came a rather hurried knocking at the front door. She opened it, and to her surprise found Flossie standing without. She was at once stricken with admiration of Flossie's hat, which was very large and apparently loaded with the contents of several beds of flowers. But Flossie herself looked to be in a state of considerable perturbation.

"Is Mr. Vance in?" she said somewhat breathlessly.

She seemed to have been hurrying, and the hat was a little on one side.

Pollyooly eyed her with some disfavour, and said coldly: "No, he isn't."

"Will he be in soon?" said Flossie anxiously.

"I don't know," said Pollyooly yet more coldly.

Flossie gazed up and down the street with a helpless air; then she said:

"Then I'd better come In and write a note for him and leave it." And she walked down the passage and into the studio.

Still wearing an air of disapproval, Pollyooly found paper and pencil for her; and she sat down and began to write. She wrote a few words, stopped, and bit the end of the pencil.

"It's dreadful when gentlemen will quarrel about you," she said in a tone and with an air in which gratified vanity forced itself firmly through the affectation of distress.

"What gentlemen?" said Pollyooly.

"Mr. Vance and my fiongsay, Mr. Reginald Butterwick," said Flossie. "I don't know how he found out that Mr. Vance is friendly with me; and I'm sure there's nothing in it—I told him so. But he's that jealous when there's a gentleman in the case that he can't believe a word I say. It isn't that he doesn't try; but he can't. He says he can't. He's got a passionate nature; he says he has. And he can't do anything with it. It runs away with him; he says it does. And now it's Mr. Vance. How he found out I can't think—unless it was something I let slip by accident about his taking me to the Chelsea Empire. He's so quick at taking you up—Reginald is; and before you know where you are, there he is—making a fuss. And what's going to happen I don't know."

Her effort to look properly distressed failed.

Pollyooly was somewhat taken aback by the flood of information suddenly gushed upon her; but she said calmly:

"But what's he going to do?"

"He's going to knock the stuffing out of Mr. Vance—he said he would. And he'll do it, too—I know he will. He's done it before. There was a gentleman friend of mine who lives in the same street as me in Hammersmith; and he got to know about him—not that there was anything to know, mind you—but he thought there was. And he blacked his eyes and made his nose bleed. You see, Reginald's a splendid boxer; he boxes at the Chiswick Polytechnic. And if he goes for Mr. Vance he'll half kill him—I know he will. Reginald's simply a terror when his blood's up."

"But Mr. Vance is very big," said Pollyooly in a doubting tone.

"But that makes no difference; bigness is nothing to a good boxer," said Flossie with an air of superior knowledge. "Mr. Butterwick says he doesn't mind taking on the biggest man in England, if he's not a boxer. And he knows that Mr. Vance isn't a boxer, because I asked him about boxing—knowing Reginald put it into my head—and he told me he didn't know a thing about it. And he'd have no chance at all against Reginald. And I let it out when I was telling Reginald that Mr. Vance was a friend of mine—only just a friend of mine—and he mustn't hurt him, and there was nothing to make a fuss about."

"I don't see why you wanted to tell him about Mr. Vance at all for, if you knew he'd make a fuss," said Pollyooly in a tone of disapproval.

"I told you it slipped out when I wasn't thinking," said Flossie, in a tone which carried no conviction; and she bent hastily to the note and added a couple of lines.

Then she broke out again in the same high-pitched, excited tone:

"And I came round here as soon as I could get away, because there wasn't any time to be lost. Reginald says he doesn't believe in losing time in anything. And he's going to take an afternoon off and come round and knock the stuffing out of Mr. Vance this very day. He can always get an afternoon off, for he's with Messrs. Mercer & Topping, and the firm has the greatest confidence in him; he says they have."

She finished the note and folded it, saying with the air which Pollyooly found hypocritical:

"It's really dreadful when gentlemen will quarrel about one so. But what am I to do? There's no way of stopping them. You'll know what it is when you get to my age—at least you would if you hadn't got red hair."

With this almost brilliantly tactful remark, she rose, gave Pollyooly the note, and adjured her to give it to Mr. Hilary Vance the moment he came in.

"What time will Mr. Butterwick get here?" said Pollyooly anxiously.

"There's no saying," said Flossie cheerfully. "But he'll get here as soon as the firm can spare him. He never loses time—Reginald doesn't."

Again she adjured Pollyooly to give Hilary Vance the note as soon as he returned, and hurried down the street to the florist's shop.

Edgar Jepson

CHAPTER III

THE INFURIATED SWAINS

Flossie's news filled Pollyooly with a considerable anxiety; but she was at a loss what to do. She knew that Hilary Vance was at the Savage Club, but she did not know whether she could reach it in time to find him there, for it was now a quarter of two. It did not seem to her a matter to be trusted to the electric telegraph; and living as she did in the old-time Temple, it never occurred to her to telephone.

There was nothing to do but await his return and give him Flossie's note of warning the moment he entered. She had been going to take the Lump for a walk on the embankment; she must postpone it. Then, unused to idleness, she cast about how she might fill up her time till his return.

She had swept and dusted the room that morning, after the departure of Mrs. Thomas, who had busied herself in them, for a short time, and ineffectually, with a dustpan, a brush, and a duster, so that there was no cleaning to be done. Presently it occurred to her that perhaps there might be some holes in the linen of her host which would be the better for her mending. A brief examination of his wardrobe showed her that her surmise was accurate: there was at least a month's hard mending to be done before that wardrobe would contain garments really worthy of the name of under-clothing. She decided to begin by darning his socks, for she chanced to have some black darning wool in her workbox. She brought three pairs of them into the studio, and began to darn. Nature had been generous, even lavish, to Hilary Vance in the matter of feet; and his socks were enormous. So were the holes in them. But their magnitude did not shake Pollyooly's resolve to darn them.

She had been at work for about three-quarters of an hour when there came a knock at the door. She went to it in some trepidation, expecting to find a raging Butterwick on the threshold. She opened it gingerly, and to her relief looked into the friendly face of Mr. James, the novelist.

On that friendly face sat the expression of weary resignation with which he was wont to intervene in the affairs of his great-hearted, but impulsive, friend.

He greeted Pollyooly warmly, and asked if Hilary Vance were in. Pollyooly told him the artist was lunching at the Savage Club.

Mr. James hesitated; then walking down the passage into the studio, he said:

"Well, I expect that you'll be able to tell me the latest news of the affair. I've just got back from Scotland to find a letter from Mr. Ruffin to say that Mr. Vance has at last found the lady of his dreams and is engaged to be married to a florist's assistant of the name of Flossie. I expect Mr. Ruffin's rotting; he knows what a bother Mr. Vance is. But I thought I'd better come round and make sure. Do you know anything about it?"

"I don't think he's engaged to her quite. But he's expecting to be every day," said Pollyooly.

"Oh, he is, is he?" said Mr. James in a tone of some exasperation. "What's she like?"

"She's fair, with a lot of fair hair and a very large hat with lots of flowers in it," said Pollyooly.

"She would be!" broke in Mr. James with a groan.

"And she gives herself airs because of that hat."

"Just what I supposed," said Mr. James, fuming.

"But she's engaged to Mr. Reginald Butterwick," said Pollyooly.

"The deuce she is!" cried Mr. James; and a faint gleam of hope brightened his face. "And who is Mr. Reginald Butterwick?"

"He's with Messrs. Mercer & Topping; but he can always get an afternoon off to knock the stuffing out of any one, because he boxes at the Chiswick Polytechnic. And he's going to get his afternoon off to-day to knock the stuffing out of Mr. Vance."

"The deuce he is!" cried Mr. James. "Well, a good hiding would do Hilary a world of good," he added in a vengeful tone. "Teach him not to go spooning florists' assistants."

"Oh, no. He might get hurt ever so badly," said Pollyooly firmly.

Mr. James' face grew stubborn; then it softened, and he said:

"Well, there's always the danger of his getting a finger broken; and that wouldn't do. I suppose we must stop the affray—it might get into the papers too."

"Yes: we must stop it, if we can," said Pollyooly anxiously.

"Well, if he's lunching at the Savage he'll play Spelka after it; and I shall catch him there. I'll keep him out all the afternoon—till his rival has tired of waiting and gone."

"Oh, yes. That would be much the best," said Pollyooly gratefully.

Mr. James went briskly to the door. At it he stopped and said:

"There's a chance that I may miss him. There may not be a game of Spelka; and he may come straight home. Perhaps you'd better wait in till about five."

"Yes: I think I'd better. He'd be sure to come back and not know anything about Mr. Butterwick, if there weren't anybody here," said Pollyooly.

He bade her good-bye; and let himself out of the house. She returned to her darning.

It was as well that she had not left the house, for about twenty minutes later the front door was opened, and the passage and studio quivered gently to Hilary Vance's weight. Pollyooly sprang up and met him at the door of the studio with Flossie's note.

At the sight of the handwriting, a large, gratified smile covered all the round expanse of his face. But as he read, the smile faded, giving way to an expression of the liveliest surprise and consternation.

Edgar Jepson

"What the deuce is this?" he cried loudly.

"She said he was going to knock the stuffing out of you, Mr. Vance, and he might be here any time this afternoon," said Pollyooly.

"And what the deuce for? What's it got to do with him?" cried Hilary Vance.

"She said he was her fiongsay," said Pollyooly, faithfully reproducing Flossie's pronunciation.

"Her fiance?" roared Hilary Vance in accents of the liveliest surprise, dismay, and horror. "Oh, woman! Woman! The faithlessness! The treachery!"

With a vast, magnificent expression of despair he dropped heavily on to the nearest chair without pausing to select a strong one. Under the stress of his emotion and his weight the chair crumpled up; and he sat down on the floor with a violence which shook the house. He sprang up, smothered, out of regard for the age and sex of Pollyooly, some language suggested by the occurrence, and with a terrific kick sent the fragments of the chair flying across the studio. Then he howled, and holding his right toes in his left hand, hopped on his left leg. He had forgotten that he was wearing thin, but patent-leather, shoes.

Then he put his feet gingerly upon the floor, ground his teeth, and roared:

"Knock the stuffing out of me, will he? I'll tear him limb from limb! The insidious villain! I'll teach him to come between me and the woman I love!"

Sad to relate Pollyooly's heart, inured to violence by her

battles with the young male inhabitants of the slum behind the Temple, where she had lodged before becoming the housekeeper of the Honourable John Ruffin, leapt joyfully at the thought of the fray, in spite of her friendship with Hilary Vance; and her quick mind grasped the fact that she might watch it in security from the door of her bedroom. Then her duty to her host came uppermost.

"But please, Mr. Vance: he's a boxer. He boxes at the Chiswick Polytechnic," she cried anxiously.

"Let him box! I'll tear him limb from limb!" roared Hilary Vance ferociously; and he strode up and down the studio, limping that he might not press heavily on his aching toes.

Pollyooly gazed at him doubtfully. Flossie's account of Mr. Butterwick's prowess had impressed her too deeply to permit her to believe that anything but painful ignominious defeat awaited Hilary Vance at his hands.

"But he blacks people's eyes and makes their noses bleed," protested Pollyooly.

"I'll tear him limb from limb!" roared Hilary Vance, still ferociously, but with less conviction in his tone.

"And he doesn't care how big anybody is, if they don't know how to box," Pollyooly insisted.

"No more do I!" roared Hilary Vance.

He stamped up and down the studio yet more vigorously since his aching toes were growing easier. Then he sank into a chair—a stronger chair—gingerly; and in a more moderate tone said:

"I'll have the scoundrel's blood. I'll teach him to cross my path."

He paused, considering the matter more coldly, and Pollyooly anxiously watched his working face. Little by little it grew calmer.

"After all it may not be the scoundrel's fault," he said in a tone of some magnanimity. "I know what women are—treachery for treachery's sake. Why should I destroy the poor wretch whose heart has probably been as scored as mine by the discovery of her treachery? He is a fellow victim."

"And perhaps you mightn't destroy him—if he's such a good boxer," said Pollyooly anxiously.

"I should certainly destroy him," said Hilary Vance with a dignified certainty. "But to what purpose? Would it give me back my unstained ideal? No. The ideal once tarnished never shines as bright again."

His face was now calm—calm and growing sorrowful. Then a sudden apprehension appeared on it:

"Besides—suppose I broke a finger—a finger of my right hand. Why should I give this blackguard a chance of maiming me?" he cried, and looked at Pollyooly earnestly.

"I don't know, Mr. Vance," said Pollyooly, answering the question in his urgent eyes.

"If I did break a finger, it might be weeks—months before I could work again. Why, I might never be able to work again!" he cried.

"That's just what Mr. James was afraid of," said Pollyooly.

"Mr. James! Has he been here?" cried Hilary Vance; and there was far more uneasiness than pleasure in his tone on thus hearing of his friend's return.

"Yes. He came to know if you were engaged yet," said Pollyooly.

"Oh, did he?" said Hilary Vance very glumly.

"Yes. And I told him you weren't."

"That's right," he said in a tone of relief.

"And he said we must stop the affray."

"He was right. It would be criminal," said Hilary Vance solemnly. "After all it isn't myself: I have to consider posterit—"

A sudden, very loud knocking on the front door cut short the word.

"That's him!" said Pollyooly in a hushed voice.

Hilary Vance rose, folded his two big arms, and faced the door of the studio, his brow knitted in a dreadful frown.

"Hadn't I better send him away?" said Pollyooly anxiously.

Hilary Vance ground his teeth and scowled steadily at the studio door for a good half-minute. Then he let his arms fall to his sides, walked with a very haughty air to his bedroom, opened the door, and from the threshold said:

"Yes: you'd better send him away—if you can."

As Pollyooly went to let the visitor in, she heard him (Mr. Vance) turn his key in the lock of his bedroom door.

It was perhaps as well that he did so; for as Pollyooly opened the front door a young man whose flashing eye proclaimed him Mr. Reginald Butterwick, pushed quickly past her and bounced into the studio.

Pollyooly followed him quickly, somewhat surprised by his size. He bounced well into the studio with an air of splendid intrepidity, which would have been more splendid had he been three or four inches higher and thicker, and uttered a snort of disappointment at its emptiness.

He turned on Pollyooly and snapped out:

"Where's your guv'ner? Where's Hilary Vance?" Pollyooly hesitated; she was still taken aback by the young man's lack of the formidable largeness Flossie had led her to expect; and she was, besides, a very truthful child. Then she said:

"I expect he's somewhere in Chelsea."

"When'll he be back?" snapped the young man.

"He's generally in to tea," with less hesitation; and she looked at him with very limpid eyes.

"He is, is he? Then I'll wait for him," said the young man in as bloodcurdling a tone as his size would allow: he did not stand five feet three in his boots.

He stood still for a moment, scowling round the studio; then he said in a dreadful tone:

"There'll be plenty of room for us."

He fell into the position of a prizefighter on guard and danced two steps to the right, and two steps to the left.

Pollyooly gazed at him earnestly. Except for his flashing eye, he was not a figure to dread, for what he lost in height he gained in slenderness. He was indeed uncommonly slender. In fact, either he had forgotten to tell Flossie that he was a featherweight boxer, or she had forgotten to pass the information on. The most terrible thing about him was his fierce air, and the most dangerous-looking his sharp, tip-tilted nose.

Then Pollyooly sat down in considerable relief; she was quite sure now that did Mr. Reginald Butterwick discover that his rival was in his bedroom and hale him forth, the person who would suffer would be Mr. Reginald Butterwick. She took up again the gigantic sock she was mending; and she kept looking up from it to observe with an easy eye the pride of the Polytechnic as he walked round the studio examining the draperies, the pictures, and the drawings on the wall. Whenever his eye rested on one signed by Hilary Vance he sniffed a bitter, contemptuous sniff. For these he had but three words of criticism; they were: "Rot!" "Rubbish!" and "Piffle!"

Once he said in a bitterly scoffing tone:

"I suppose your precious guv'ner thinks he's got the artistic temperament."

"I don't know," said Pollyooly.

He squared briskly up to an easel, danced lightly on his toes before it, and said:

"I'll give him the artistic temperament all right."

At last he paused in his wanderings before the industrious Pollyooly, and his eyes fell on the gigantic sock she was darning. She saw his expression change; something of the fierce confidence of the intrepid boxer passed out of his face.

"I say, what's that you're darning?" he said quickly.

"It's a sock," said Pollyooly.

"It looks more like a sack than a sock. Whose sock is it?" said Mr. Reginald Butterwick; and there was a faint note of anxiety in his tone.

"It's Mr. Vance's sock," said Pollyooly; and with gentle pride she held it up in a fashion to display its full proportions.

Mr. Reginald Butterwick took two or three nervous steps to the right, looking askance at the sock as he moved. It was not really as large as a sack.

"Big man, your guv'ner? Eh?" he said in a finely careless tone.

"I should think he was!" cried Pollyooly with enthusiasm.

Mr. Reginald Butterwick looked still more earnestly at the sock and said:

"One of those tall lanky chaps—eh?"

"He's tall, but he isn't lanky—not a bit," said Pollyooly quickly. "He's tremendously big—broad and thick as well as tall, you know. He's more like a giant than a man."

"Oh, I know those giants—flabby—flabby," said Mr. Reginald Butterwick; and he laughed a short, scoffing laugh which rang uneasy.

"He's not flabby!" cried Pollyooly indignantly. "He's tremendously strong. Why—why—when he heard you were coming he smashed that chair and kicked it into the corner just because he was annoyed."

Mr. Reginald Butterwick looked at the smallish fragments of the chair in the corner; and his face became the face of a quiet, respectable clerk.

"He did, did he?" he said coldly.

"Yes, and he wanted to tear you limb from limb. He said so," said Pollyooly.

"That's a game two can play at," said Mr. Reginald Butterwick; but his tone lacked conviction.

"Oh, he'd do it—quite easily," said Pollyooly confidently.

Mr. Reginald Butterwick stared at her and then at the sock. He opened his mouth to speak and then shut it again. Then he whistled a short, defiant whistle which went out of tune toward the end. Then he walked the length of the studio and back. Then he stopped and said to Pollyooly very fiercely:

"Do you think I've got nothing else to do but wait here all the afternoon for your precious guv'ner to come home to tea?"

"I don't know," said Pollyooly politely.

"Well, I have—plenty," said Mr. Reginald Butterwick savagely.

Pollyooly said nothing.

"And what's more, I'm going to do it!" said Mr. Reginald Butterwick yet more savagely; and he strode firmly to the door. On the threshold he paused and added: "But you tell your guv'ner from me—Mr. Reginald Butterwick—that he hasn't seen the last of me—not by a long chalk. One of these fine nights when he's messing round with—well, you tell him what I've told you—that's all. He'll know."

With that he passed through the door and banged it heavily behind him. The front door was larger and heavier, so that he was able to bang it more loudly still.

CHAPTER IV

THE DUCHESS HAS AN IDEA

Pollyooly heaved a sigh as the studio trembled to the shock of the banged front door, a sigh chiefly of relief, but tinged also with a faint regret that she had not seen Mr. Reginald Butterwick torn limb from limb. She knew that she would not really have enjoyed the sight; and the mess in the cleaned studio would have been exceedingly annoying; but there were primitive depths in her heart, and somewhere in them was the regret that she had missed the thrilling spectacle.

The studio still quivered to the bang, the sigh still trembled on Pollyooly's lip, when the bedroom door opened, and Hilary Vance came forth with an immense scowl on his spacious face and said fiercely:

"So the scoundrel's gone, has he?"

"Yes. When I told him how big you were, he didn't seem so eager to fight. And he went away," said Pollyooly quickly. "But he told me to tell you that you hadn't seen the last of him—not by a long chalk."

Her host's scowl lightened a little; there was almost a faint satisfaction on his face as he said:

"So he fears my rivalry still, does he?" Then his face grew gloomier than ever; and he added: "There's no need. I am not one to sit at the feet of a tarnished ideal. There will be a gap—there is a gap—but I have done with HER for good and all. I have—done—with—HER."

He had drawn himself up to utter the last words with a splendid air; then he said sadly:

"I think I should like my tea."

"I'll get it at once," said Pollyooly cheerfully.

She was not long about it. Hilary Vance took the Lump on his knee, gave him a lump of sugar, poured out the tea, and began to drink it with an air of gloomy resignation.

Presently he patted the Lump's bright red curls and said:

"Let this be a warning to you, red cherub, never to trust a woman—never as long as you live."

The Lump grunted peacefully.

"He's too young to understand, or it wouldn't be right to teach him such a thing as that," said Pollyooly in a tone of disapproval.

"Not right?" cried Hilary Vance stormily. "But you've seen for yourself! You've seen how that girl led me on to squander the treasure of a splendid passion on her unresponsive spirit while, all the time, she was abasing herself before a miserable, preposterous scoundrel like that ruffian Butterwick."

"He was rather small," said Pollyooly thoughtfully. "But I daresay he'd make her a good husband. He looked quite respectable."

"A good husband!" cried Hilary Vance with a dreadful sneer.

"But I expect she'll lead him a life. She looked like it," said Pollyooly, thoughtfully pursuing the subject.

"Serve him right!" cried Hilary Vance with terrible scorn. "He has learnt her treachery to me; and if he marries her after that, he deserves all he gets. If she betrays my trust, she'll betray his."

Pollyooly was silent, considering the matter. Then, summing it up, she said with conviction:

"I don't think she's the kind of girl to trust at all."

"I must have been blind—blind," said Hilary Vance.

Then came the sound of a taxicab drawing up before the house, and then a knocking at the front door. Pollyooly opened it, and found Mr. James on the threshold. He looked uncommonly anxious and said quickly:

"I missed him. Has he come back?"

"Yes; he's having his tea."

"And this fellow Butterwick?" said Mr. James.

"Oh, he came; and then, when he found how big Mr. Vance is, he went away. But he hasn't done with Mr. Vance—not by a long chalk. He told me to tell him so," said Pollyooly.

"Well, I'm glad they didn't scrap," said Mr. James in a tone of relief. "If they didn't at once, they're not very likely to later."

"Oh, no: they won't now," said Pollyooly confidently. "You see as soon as he heard that Mr. Butterwick was her—her fiongsay"—she hesitated over the word because Hilary Vance had shaken her original conception of its pronunciation—"he gave her up for good."

"That is a blessing," said the novelist in a tone of yet greater relief.

He had been looking forward to a disagreeable and very likely hopeless struggle with his friend's infatuation.

He walked down the passage and into the studio briskly. But not quickly enough to prevent an expression of funereal gloom flooding Hilary Vance's face.

"How are you?" said Mr. James cheerfully.

"In the depths—in the depths—my last illusion shattered," said the artist in the gloomiest kind of despairing croak.

"Oh, you never know," said Mr. James.

"I shall never trust a woman again—never," said the artist in an inexorable tone.

"But I thought you'd given up trusting them months ago," said Mr. James in considerable surprise.

"I was deceived—this one seemed so different. She was a serpent—a veritable serpent," said Hilary Vance in his deepest tone.

"Yes. They are apt to be like that," said Mr. James with some carelessness. "May I have some tea?"

Gloomily the artist poured him out a cup of tea; gloomily he watched him drink it. Heedless of his gloom, Mr. James plunged into an account of his stay in Scotland, telling of the country, the food, and the people with an agreeable, racy vivacity. Slowly the great cloud lifted from Hilary Vance's ample face. He grew interested; he asked questions; at last he said firmly:

"I must go to Scotland. Nature—Nature pure and undenied is what my seared soul needs."

"It wouldn't be a bad idea," said Mr. James.

"I shall wear a kilt," said Hilary Vance solemnly. "The winds of heaven playing round my legs would assist healing nature; and I must be in complete accord with the country."

"A kilt wouldn't be a bad idea," said Mr. James.

Hilary Vance paused and appeared to be thinking deeply; then he said:

"The Scotch peasant lassies, James—are they as attractive nowadays as they appear to have been in the days of Burns?"

"I thought you'd done with women!" cried Mr. James.

"I *have* done with women," said the poet with cold sternness. "I have done with the cold-hearted, treacherous, meretricious women of the town. But the simple, trusting and trustworthy country girl, the daughter of the soil, in perpetual touch with nature—surely communion with her would be healing too."

"Oh, hang it all!" said Mr. James quite despondently.

Hilary Vance plunged once more into deep thought; then he said:

"Where does one buy a kilt—and a sporran?"

"Whiteley's, I suppose," said Mr. James. Then he added hastily: "But I say, oughtn't we to do something to amuse these children?"

At once his friend forgot his seared heart; for the while the process of healing it did not exercise his wits. He flung himself heart and soul into the business of amusing Pollyooly and the Lump; and presently the studio rang with their screams of joy. There may have been some truth in the assertion of his detractors that Hilary Vance's drawing was facile and too far on the side of mere prettiness; but no one in the world could deny that he made a splendid elephant: his trumpeting was especially true to life.

Ten days passed pleasantly at his studio; and both Pollyooly and the Lump were the better for the change. Three times she went to the King's Bench Walk and cleaned the rooms against the Honourable John Ruffin's return; four times she went to the dancing class in Soho, where she was training for a career on the stage. On the evening of the tenth day came a letter to say that he would be back at noon on the morrow. After breakfast, therefore, Hilary Vance despatched the two children back to the King's Bench Walk in a taxicab, the Lump hugging a large box of chocolate creams, Pollyooly, in no less joy, clasping firmly her shabby little purse which contained, beyond the silver she carried to meet any natural expense, a golden sovereign, the artist's parting gift. Her sky was now serene; but she was still mindful of the days when the jaws of the workhouse had yawned for her and the Lump, and she lost no chance of adding to her hoard in the Post Office Savings Bank. Immediately on her arrival at the

Temple she went to the post office and added the sovereign to it.

The Honourable John Ruffin arrived from Buda-Pesth, looking the browner for the change, and in very good spirits. He brought the friendliest messages and Hungarian gifts to Pollyooly and the Lump from the Esmeralda, and was able to assure them that she was in excellent health, and enjoying a genuine triumph.

When he had delivered the Esmeralda's gifts and assured Pollyooly of her prosperity, there came a short silence; then Pollyooly said:

"And the Moldo-Wallachian, sir?"

The fine grey eyes of the Honourable John Ruffin twinkled, as he said gravely:

"The Moldo-Wallachian has returned to Moldo-Wallachia. When the ideal was once more clearly presented to the Esmeralda, the attractions of the Moldo-Wallachian faded as flowers fade in a drought."

"I'm glad she isn't going to marry a foreigner," said Pollyooly with true patriotism.

"She would never be happy in Moldo-Wallachia," said the Honourable John Ruffin with conviction.

"Oh, no, sir," said Pollyooly.

There was a pause; then he said:

"And how did you leave Mr. Vance?"

"Oh, he was all right, sir," said Pollyooly.

"Oh, he was, was he? Did you by any chance come across a young lady of the name of Flossie while you were staying at Chelsea?"

"Yes, sir. But he doesn't have anything to do with her now, sir. He goes past the shop with an air of cold dignity—he says he does; and he's going to Scotland to wear a kilt to get quite cured—he says he is," said Pollyooly quickly.

"It sounds most efficacious," said the Honourable John Ruffin. "But how did it all happen?"

Pollyooly told the story of the intervention of Mr. Butterwick; and the Honourable John Ruffin chuckled freely, for no reason that she could see, as he listened to it. At the end of it he said sententiously:

"Well, all's well that ends well. These foreign countries are not suited to English girls: Miss Flossie would never be happy in Bohemia."

The next morning, when she brought in his grilled bacon, he said that they might now congratulate themselves on the prospect of leading their quiet, industrious lives in peace for a while.

These congratulations, however, were premature, for only three days later he was sitting in his rooms, having just come from the Law Courts, where he had been acting as junior counsel in an awkward case, and was bracing himself to the effort of getting himself his afternoon tea, since Pollyooly had gone with the Lump to take the air in Hyde Park.

Suddenly there came a sharp, hurried knocking on his outer door.

The Honourable John Ruffin raised his eyebrows, opened his eyes rather wide, and said to his cigarette:

"A woman in distress, evidently. Who on earth can it be?"

He did not spring to his feet and dash to the door to offer instant aid to the distressed one. He rose slowly and walked slowly to the door, assuming slowly as he went an air of deep, but patient, resignation.

He opened the door gingerly. On the threshold stood the beautiful, high-spirited and wilful Duchess of Osterley.

"Caroline, by Jove! Why, I thought you were out of England, still hiding Marion from Osterley," he cried, and smiled with pleasure at the sight of her beautiful face.

The Duke and Duchess of Osterley had been at daggers drawn for nearly two years; and since both of them had sought to bring their feud forcibly to an end in the Law Courts, the Anglo-Saxon peoples had had no cause to complain of any lack of effort on their part to be entertaining. The upshot of the law proceedings had been that the Court, with a futility almost fatuous, had ordered the duchess to return to her husband, and, what was far more important, had given the custody of their little daughter of twelve, Lady Marion Ricksborough, to the duke.

The Anglo-Saxon peoples felt that the duke had scored heavily; and the duchess agreed with them. She was not one to sit submissive under defeat; and presently those peoples read with the liveliest interest and pleasure that she had carried off her daughter and hidden her with such skill that the detectives, official and unofficial, had failed utterly to find her.

In this carrying off and hiding Pollyooly had played the important part. It had been a freak of nature to make her and Lady Marion Ricksborough so closely alike, that even when they were together it was hard to tell which was which. The duchess had taken advantage of this likeness to substitute Pollyooly for Lady Marion at Ricksborough Court, the duke's chief country seat, for a fortnight.

The duke, Lady Marion's nurse, and her governess had believed Lady Marion Ricksborough to be still with them, and had given the duchess all the time she needed to hide her.

For a whole fortnight Pollyooly had played her part with such skill that only the duke's nephew and heir, Lord Ronald Ricksborough, had discovered that she was not Lady Marion. A most discreet boy of fourteen, and already Pollyooly's warm friend, he was the last person to spoil the sport; and at the end of the fortnight she had slipped away and returned by motor car to her post of housekeeper to the Honourable John Ruffin and Mr. Gedge-Tomkins in the King's Bench Walk.

Ignorant of the fact that Lady Marion Ricksborough had fled a fortnight previously, the detectives, both official and private, had taken up the search for her from the moment of Pollyooly's disappearance from the Court. It is hardly a matter for wonder that they did not go far along a trail which had been cold for a fortnight.

As he said, the Honourable John Ruffin had believed the duchess to be hiding out of England; and he showed himself unfeignedly pleased to see her. He put her in his most comfortable chair, made her take off her hat, and said:

"Now, I'll make you some tea."

The Honourable John Ruffin went to the kitchen; the duchess rose restlessly and followed him. As he made the tea he lectured her on the importance of making it not only with boiling water, but with water which had not been boiling for more than a quarter of a minute, and that poured on to a fine China tea in a warmed pot without taking the kettle right off the stove.

The rebellious duchess, impatient to tell him the object of her visit, made several faces at him; and twice she said contemptuously:

"You and your old tea!"

But when she came to drink it, she admitted handsomely that it was better than she could have made it herself.

She drank it; grew suddenly serious, and said:

"John, I'm in a mess, and I've come to you for help."

"It is yours to the half of my fortune—at present about fourteen shillings," said the Honourable John Ruffin warmly.

"Well, I didn't take Marion abroad," said the duchess. "They always look abroad for people who bolt. I borrowed Pinky Wallerton's car and drove her down, myself, to a cottage I bought in Devonshire—in the pinewoods above Budleigh Salterton."

"That sounds all right."

"It was—quite—till this morning. Then, without a word of warning, at eleven o'clock, one of Osterley's lawyers turned up with a detective."

"And got her?"

"No. Fortunately she was out in the wood with her nurse. I gave Eglantine, my maid, twenty pounds and told her to get quietly to Marion while I kept the brutes in play, rush her down to the station, and catch the London train. They'd just time if they ran most of the way."

"But the lawyer would only have to wire to Osterley to meet the train at Waterloo," said the Honourable John Ruffin.

"I thought of that," said the duchess quickly. "I told her to leave the express at Salisbury, go on to Woking by a slow train, take a taxi from there to my old nurse's, Mrs. Simpson's, in Camden Town, and leave Marion with her."

"Excellent," said the Honourable John Ruffin in warm approval.

"Then she's to come on here with Marion's clothes in time to catch the six o'clock to Exeter from Paddington."

"Here? With Marion's clothes? What for?" said the Honourable John Ruffin.

"Why, to put on Mary Bride—Pollyooly as you call her. I want to borrow her again, substitute her for Marion, and let her keep the brutes quiet while I carry Marion off to a cottage I have bought in the north of Scotland for just such an emergency as this."

The Honourable John Ruffin sprang to his feet with flashing eyes:

"What? Rob me of my bacon-griller again? The last time my breakfast was spoilt for a fortnight. You don't know what you ask!" he cried in tones in which indignation and horror were nicely blended.

"Oh, but this won't be for a fortnight—a couple of days at the outside. Surely you could eat fish for breakfast for a couple of mornings," pleaded the duchess.

"I never eat fish for breakfast," said the Honourable John Ruffin coldly. "I am an Englishman and a patriot—eggs and bacon."

"But just for once," said the duchess.

The hard expression faded slowly from his face; he took a turn up and down the room; then he said in a tone of infinite sadness:

"Well, well, I suppose I must sacrifice myself again. What a thing it is to be a cousin! But how are you going to work it? Surely you're being followed?"

"Rather," said the duchess cheerfully. "But I don't take Mary Bride with me. I go back to Budleigh Salterton by the four forty-five from Waterloo; and my follower will no doubt go with me. Eglantine and Mary Bride will go down to Exeter by the six o'clock from Paddington, motor over, and slip into the house late at night. There's sure to be some one watching it; and once they believe Marion to be in it, they'll go on watching it without bothering about me. I only want to be left alone for six hours, and I'll get Marion away without leaving a trace."

"Strategist," said the Honourable John Ruffin in a tone of admiring approval. "I hope you'll pull it off. You deserve to for having thought it out so thoroughly. Fortunately, Pollyooly is due home at a quarter of five, so there'll be no trouble there. She's the most punctual person in the Temple."

"That's lucky," said the duchess with a sigh of thankfulness.

There was nothing more to be arranged; and if she were going to catch her train comfortably, it was time that she started for Waterloo. He escorted her to Fleet Street, put her into a taxicab, and bade her good-bye.

The taxicab started; he turned to return to his rooms, stopped short, and said sharply:

"Bother! I forgot to arrange about Pollyooly's salary!"

CHAPTER V

POLLYOOLY IS CALLED IN

On his way back to the King's Bench Walk the Honourable John Ruffin pondered this matter of salary and came to the conclusion that five pounds would not be too high a fee for the duchess to pay for skilled work of this kind. He must remember to tell Eglantine to tell her to give Pollyooly that sum.

Pollyooly was rather earlier than he had expected: at five and twenty minutes to five he heard her latchkey in the lock of his outer door, and when it opened he called to her to come to him.

She entered leading the Lump. His red hair was a rather brighter red than the hair of Pollyooly; but his eyes were of the same deep blue and his clear skin of the same paleness. They would have made a charming picture of Cupid led by an angel child.

"Ah, Pollyooly!" said the Honourable John Ruffin cheerfully. "You are about to realise the truth of those immortal lines:

"Oh, what a tangled web we weave
When first we practice to deceive!"

"Please, sir, I haven't been deceiving any one," said Pollyooly, knitting her brow in a faint anxiety.

"Not recently, perhaps. But you have deceived. You deceived the Duke of Osterley by taking the place of his daughter."

"Oh, him?" said Pollyooly in a very care-free tone; and her face grew serene.

"You don't seem to feel it much," said the Honourable John Ruffin sadly. "But now you are called on to deceive lawyers and detectives."

"Am I to be Lady Marion again?" said Pollyooly quickly.

"You are, indeed," said the Honourable John Ruffin.

"And shall I be paid again for doing it?"

Her angel face flushed, and her blue eyes danced.

"Certainly you will be paid. I am going to tell Eglantine, the duchess's maid, to see to it. She's coming for you, and you haven't any time to lose. She's going to take you down to Devonshire by the train which leaves Paddington at six," said the Honourable John Ruffin.

"Then I'd better take the Lump round to Mrs. Brown at once," said Pollyooly; and her eyes sparkled and danced.

"You had," said the Honourable John Ruffin. "It's only for a couple of nights at the outside, tell her."

"And that's quite as long as I like to leave him," she said in a tone of complete satisfaction; and she ran briskly up-stairs to their attic for the Lump's sleeping-suit.

She was not long taking him to Mrs. Brown, who lived in the little slum, the last remnant of Alsatia, behind the King's Bench Walk; and she welcomed him warmly. Pollyooly and he had lodged with her before they had gone to live in the King's Bench Walk, and Mrs. Brown had grown very fond of him. She had taken charge of him during the time Pollyooly had spent at Ricksborough Court and was delighted to have him with her again. Also she was disengaged for the next two days and was able to take charge of the housekeeping at number 75 the King's Bench Walk during Pollyooly's absence.

Pollyooly had not been gone five minutes, when there came a gentle knocking at the door of the Honourable John Ruffin's chambers. He opened it to find Eglantine, a pretty, dark, slim girl of twenty-two, standing on the doormat, carrying a small kitbag and wearing an air of deepest mystery.

"You're Mademoiselle Eglantine, I suppose?" he said.

"Ye—es. And you are Monsieur Ruffin," she whispered with an air of utter secrecy. "Ze duchess she 'av been 'ere?"

"She has. Come on in. Pollyooly is making preparations to go with you," said the Honourable John Ruffin briskly. "She'll be here in a few minutes."

He stepped aside for her to pass. She looked back down the staircase carefully and with the greatest caution; then she entered and went on tiptoe, noiselessly, down the passage into the sitting-room. There could be no doubt that she was thoroughly enjoying the part of a conspirator and resolved to play it to the limit.

The Honourable John Ruffin was the last man in the world to

Edgar Jepson

spoil her simple pleasure, and as they came into the sitting-room he suddenly gripped her arm.

Eglantine jumped and squeaked.

"Hist!" said the Honourable John Ruffin, laying a finger on his lips, frowning portentously, and rolling his eyes. Then he added in blank verse, as being appropriate to the conspiratorial attitude: "I thought I heard a footstep on the stairs."

They both listened intently—at least Eglantine did; she hardly breathed in her intentness. Then he said in a declamatory fashion:

"I was mistaken; we are saved again."

He loosed her arm. She breathed more easily, tapped the kit-bag, and said:

"I 'av brought ze Lady Marion's clo'es."

"Good," said the Honourable John Ruffin. "Sit down."

She sat down, breathing quickly, gazing earnestly at the Honourable John Ruffin, who folded his arms and wore his best darkling air.

Presently Pollyooly's key grated in the lock.

"Hist! She comes!" said the Honourable John Ruffin.

Eglantine rose, quivering.

Pollyooly came in, shut the door sharply behind her, and came briskly down the passage into the sitting-room.

At the sight of her Eglantine forgot the whispering caution of the conspirator; she cried loudly:

"But ze likeness! Eet ees marvellous! Incredible! Eet ees 'er leetle ladyship exact!"

"Yes. And she'll be more like her than ever in her clothes. Hurry up and get her into them," said the Honourable John Ruffin briskly.

He bustled them up the stairs to Pollyooly's attic; and as Eglantine helped her into Lady Marion Ricksborough's clothes, she continued to express her lively wonder at the likeness. She was not long making the change, and they came quickly downstairs. But the Honourable John Ruffin would not let them start at once.

"It's no use your getting there too early and hanging about the station," he said firmly. "That's when you'd get spotted. You want to get there just about three minutes before the train starts. You've no luggage to bother you."

He made both of them eat some cake, and gave Eglantine a glass of wine with it, for he thought that she needed something to steady her excited nerves. Then he told her that the duchess was to pay Pollyooly a fee of five pounds, and bade Pollyooly be sure to wire to him the time of the train by which she was returning to London.

Then he decided that it was time for them to start, and wished them good luck. He did not go with them, for he did not wish to be seen by any one taking an active part in the affairs of the Duke and Duchess of Osterley.

In the taxicab Eglantine was eloquent on the matter of the charm and distinction of the Honourable John Ruffin: plainly he had made a deep impression on her. But when they reached the station she resumed the striking manners of a conspirator so admirably that in the three minutes she spent paying the taxi-driver and buying tickets she attracted the keen attention of two of the detectives of the railway. They followed her, as she tiptoed about with hunched shoulders, and watched her with the eyes of lynxes; but she puzzled them. They assured one another that she had some game on (their knowledge of fallen human nature was too exact for them to miss that fact) but for the life of them they could not discover, or guess, what it was.

On the platform she chose an empty compartment and stood before the door of it for a good half-minute, looking up and down the train with eyes even more lynxlike than those of the detectives. Then she almost flung Pollyooly into the carriage, hustled her into the farthest corner, and fairly sat on her in her effort to screen her from the eyes of the crowd.

"Do not stir!" she hissed. "Ze train veel soon start! Zen we are saved!"

Pollyooly could not have stirred, had she wished, so firmly did Eglantine crush her into the corner. One of the detectives came to the window and stared into the carriage gloomily. Eglantine met his gaze with steady eyes. The guard whistled and waved his flag; the detective fell back. He said to his colleague that it was a rum go. The train started.

As their carriage passed out of the station, with a deep sigh of relief Eglantine relaxed to an easier, less crushing posture, and at once took up the subject of the Honourable John Ruffin. She showed herself exceedingly curious about him, and Pollyooly's natural discretion was somewhat strained in answering her questions. It was difficult to convey as little information as possible.

But at the end of half an hour Eglantine had exhausted that subject; and she turned to the yet more interesting matter of her own affairs. She had much to tell Pollyooly about Devonshire, the wet garden of England. Its horticultural advantages seemed to weigh but lightly with her; she dwelt chiefly on the loneliness of the life she had been leading, and deplored bitterly the fact that its inglorious ease was spoiling her figure by increasing her girth.

Then, with an air of mystery and in deeper tones, she confided to Pollyooly that her lot in this wet desert was not without its alleviation. A wealthy landowner (he did own a part of the market-garden he so sedulously cultivated) had developed a grand—oh, but a grand!—passion for her, and was positively persecuting her with his honourable intentions.

Pollyooly was deeply interested by her tale, for her recent experience with Mr. Hilary Vance, Mr. Reginald Butterwick and Flossie had forced the tender passion on her attention. She was greatly puzzled by the reason which Eglantine gave for not making her landowner happy by marrying him, that he was bearded. Mrs. Brown's husband, a cheerful police-man, was bearded; but they were uncommonly happy together. In the end she made up her mind that Eglantine's feeling in the matter must be a French prejudice.

They reached Exeter at a few minutes past ten; and having no luggage but the little kit-bag, in a few minutes, in spite of the conspiratorial air and behaviour of Eglantine, they were speeding swiftly in the motor car toward Budleigh Salterton. It was a delightful, moonlit night, and Pollyooly enjoyed the drive greatly.

About forty minutes later the car stopped at a little gate leading into a pine wood, and they descended, bade the

Edgar Jepson

driver good night, and went through it. In the path through the dark wood Eglantine lost her air of competent and excited leadership. She was timorous, held Pollyooly tightly by the arm, and when a bird, or an animal, rustled in the bushes, she squeaked.

At last the path ended in a little gate opening into the garden of the lonely house. They came up to it very gently, and Eglantine peered round the garden, searching for the lawyer and the detective.

It seemed empty, and as she opened the gate she whispered:

"We must roon quick!"

They bolted across the garden to the back door, and as they reached it a man burst out of the bushes twenty yards on their left, and dashed at them. Eglantine screamed, but she opened the door, dragged Pollyooly through it, slammed the door in the pursuer's face, and shot the bolt. At the sound of the bang the duchess came flying through the lighted hall. At the sight of Pollyooly she cried:

"Thank goodness you've come!"

Eglantine burst into an excited narrative of their journey and narrow escape from the watcher in the garden.

"Then he actually saw Mary Bride come into the house?" cried the duchess joyfully, and she clapped her hands.

"But yes! Ever so plainly!" cried Eglantine.

"Good! Nothing could be better!" said the duchess. "They'll think that Marion is in the house, and that's all I want."

She kissed Pollyooly, thanked her for coming, asked if the journey had tired her very much, and led her into the dining-room, where a delicious supper awaited her. As she ate it the duchess, watching her with an air of lively satisfaction, matured her plans. At last she said:

"I was going to let them catch you to-morrow morning, and then I was going up to London with you. But you look like a clever little girl; do you think you could hide in the wood from them all the morning? If you could, I would go up to London first thing, and I should have lots of time to get away with Marion before they caught you and found out who you were."

"Oh, yes! I'm sure I could!" cried Pollyooly eagerly; and her eyes shone with a bright joy at the prospect of so excellent a game of hide-and-seek. "If once I got into that wood, they'd never find me unless I let them. Only it would be a good deal easier if I wore a dark frock."

"You shall!" cried the duchess. "It would be perfectly splendid! I know you're a clever little girl. Otherwise you couldn't have made them believe for so long at Ricksborough Court that you were Marion. Cook shall make you up a packet of sandwiches so that you won't starve; and if you can keep them busy till the afternoon, we shall have all the time we want to get comfortably away."

"I think I can," said Pollyooly with the confidence born of much experience in hide-and-seek. "But even if they do catch me, they won't know I'm not Lady Marion; I'm sure I can keep them from bothering you all day."

The duchess kissed her again, and said:

"I shall be ever so much obliged to you if you do. But half a day will be quite enough. And now you'd better go to bed; you must be sleepy, and the more sleep you get the fresher you'll be to-morrow. I shall be gone long before you're up."

She took her up-stairs to Marion's bedroom, a charming room on the first floor, and Pollyooly found the most comfortable spring bed so lulling that in spite of her expectation of an exciting morrow, she soon fell asleep.

The yet more excited duchess was longer falling asleep; but she rose at half-past five and dressed and breakfasted. It was a quarter past six when she came out into the garden, on her way to the station, and found the detective sunning himself, after the chill of his night-watch, on the garden fence at a point from which he had under observation both the path to the front door and that to the back. He had a rather heavy face, but he showed a proper sense of her rank and position, for he rose and raised his hat nearly three inches, respectfully.

A woman of the world, the duchess knew the advantage of his having a tale to think upon, for she said with a nice show of indignation:

"I'm going straight to my solicitor in town to take the final steps to have this persecution stopped! I'm going to have you removed by the police. You enter this house and touch my little girl at your own risk! I've warned you."

"Yes, your Grace. Quite so, your Grace. It'll be all right, your Grace," said the detective, sleepily vague, but anxious to propitiate.

The duchess walked briskly down to the station.

CHAPTER VI

POLLYOOLY PLAYS HER FAVOURITE PART

At half-past eight Eglantine, already bubbling, in spite of the earliness of the hour, with excited animation, awoke Pollyooly and pulled up the blind of the bedroom window.

Then she cried:

"'E ees 'ere! Queek! Queek! Coom to ze window! Let 'im see you!"

Pollyooly jumped out of bed and ran to the window. The detective stood on the lawn regarding the house gloomily. At the sight of her face he beamed sleepily.

Eglantine laughed and cried:

"Good! Now 'e zinks you are 'ere! But you must eat your breakfast queek, and be ready to run fast into ze wood when ze lawyer coom!"

Pollyooly bathed and dressed quickly, putting on a dark frock that she might be less visible in the thickets. Then she came briskly down-stairs and made an excellent breakfast.

She was just finishing it when Eglantine, on the watch at the window, cried:

"'Ere is ze lawyer! You must fly! Oh, but queek!"

Pollyooly seized a cap and the packet of sandwiches which lay ready to hand, and as she put on the cap she saw the lawyer, a middle-aged, but stout gentleman, conferring with the detective and smiling triumphantly and rubbing his hands at the news of her presence in the house. She smiled too—a smile of pleasant anticipation. But then, as the lawyer walked to the front door, the detective walked briskly to the back, and she frowned.

"Oh, bothaire! What are we to do?" cried Eglantine.

"Isn't there a window I could get out of?" said Pollyooly quickly.

"But yes! Coom quick!" cried Eglantine, running out of the room.

Pollyooly hurried after her; and there came the loud rat-tat of the lawyer at the front door. They ran into the drawing-room and Eglantine opened the window gently. The detective knocked at the back door; the lawyer knocked again, louder. Pollyooly leaned out of the window, weighing her chances. She saw that to get to the little gate into the wood she would have to pass the detective. But on her left, in the fence of the wood, was a gap which had been filled by a post and rails. Though it would bring her in sight of the lawyer at the front door, that seemed the safer way, since he was stouter, and probably less swift of foot than the detective. She climbed out of the window and made a dash for it. She reached the fence, went over it like a cat; and her foot already touched the ground on the other side as the lawyer saw her, and in his indignation and surprise howled like a skelped hound.

He was more used to office work than action; and it was fully five seconds before he started for the wood. In those five seconds Pollyooly had gone a good thirty yards into it. He rushed for the post and rails, and climbed them with his eyes nearly starting out of his head in his anxiety to see her. Then, instead of trying to hear in which direction she was moving, he stood on the fence and bellowed to the detective to come to him.

The detective, tired by his night watch, was slow in grasping what had happened. By the time he had reached the lawyer, had learned that Pollyooly had taken to the woods, and was himself over the fence, many valuable seconds had been lost; and Pollyooly, who had turned sharply to the left, was sixty yards down the wood, moving noiselessly, out of hearing.

She threaded the mazes of the wood swiftly, with straining ears, marking the loud rustling of her pursuers in the undergrowth. It grew fainter and fainter, for they plunged on straight ahead of them; and then it died quite away. She went on slowly, enjoying the wood, the fragrance of the flowers, and the song of the birds in the sun-flecked glades.

About twenty minutes later she heard again the rustling of her pursuers, faint and far away, but drawing nearer. She moved along before it, and came to a gate opening into a leafy lane. Below, about a mile away, lay the town of Budleigh Salterton, and the sea, shining in the sun.

She climbed on to the gate to get a better view (she had time enough), her active brain working swiftly. She perceived that there were even pleasanter ways of spending a summer's day in Devonshire than playing hide-and-seek in a wood with a lawyer and a detective. Then she cast one look back into the green depths of the wood, slipped over the gate, and bolted down the lane as hard as she could run. Her only task had been to keep the lawyer and the detective busy during the morning; and she thought that the wood might be trusted to keep them busy without any help from her. Eight minutes later she arrived, panting, in the High Street of the town, slowed down, and strolled to the beach.

But the lawyer and the detective ranged the wood like questing hounds.

As she came on to the esplanade a very large gentleman in grey flannel was so impressed by her flower-like, angel face that, without pausing to cast about for an introduction, he entered into conversation with her. She was very affable with him, but not wholly open; for after a while she left him under the impression that, so far from being an orphan, she was staying with her parents in lodgings in the station road. But she bore away from their colloquy a pleasing shilling with which he had invited her to buy chocolate.

She walked along the esplanade somewhat disappointed that the beach should all of it be large pebbles. She had always believed the shore of the sea to be sand. She did not, however, repine, but walked along to the end of it, watching the bathers and the playing children, in a great content. Then she went down the path beyond the esplanade, between the sea and marshes, to the mouth of the swift-flowing Otter. She walked out over the slippery rocks to the edge of the ebbing sea, and finding some children paddling about in a pool, joined them.

And still the lawyer and the detective ranged the wood like questing hounds.

The pleasant feel of the warm salt water on her legs inspired

Pollyooly with larger desires. She put on her shoes and stockings and came back to the esplanade. She soon learned that a bathing-dress and a bathing-machine could be hired. She hired them and bathed. She bathed for a long time, a longer time than was good for her.

And still the lawyer and the detective ranged the wood like questing hounds.

At last she tore herself from the water, dressed, and lay on the warm pebbles, drying her beautiful red hair in the sun. The church clock struck twelve; slowly, but with a good appetite, she ate her sandwiches—chicken sandwiches.

And still the lawyer and the detective ranged the wood like questing hounds.

After her lunch Pollyooly bought herself a bottle of lemonade at a confectioner's shop in the High Street; then once more she sought the mouth of the Otter. There, hunting among the rocks, paddling, watching the sea-gulls on the red cliffs beyond the stream, she enjoyed herself greatly. It is to be doubted that a happier child could have been found out of London.

The lawyer and the detective no longer ranged the wood like questing hounds. They had already done all the ranging the weather permitted. Moreover, the lawyer was not of sleuth-hound build, and the chase had reddened his face almost to the colour of the carapace of a boiled lobster. Unfortunately his face was not of the durable texture of a carapace; and the skin was peeling off his nose.

They had returned to the pretty garden from which they had started on their quest; and the detective had gone into the town to get the food he needed so badly and to bring back lunch for the lawyer. The lawyer sat on a bench, awaiting his return impatiently. Searching the wood like a questing hound had given him also a fine appetite.

It was soon after two o'clock that Pollyooly made the acquaintance of the boy Edward, or the boy Edward made the acquaintance of Pollyooly. It is difficult to be sure how these things happened. But both of them were lonely; Pollyooly was of far too simple and direct a nature to be much hampered by the cold conventions of a sophisticated civilisation; and Edward was but ten.

For all his extreme youth, he was an agreeable companion; and so it came about that Pollyooly, who had meant to return to the house at three o'clock, was detained by Edward and the sea till half-past four. She was not loth to be detained; she was indeed pleased to be giving the duchess her full measure of hours, and the lawyer and detective a really good run for their money.

But as a matter of fact they did no running at all that afternoon. At three o'clock the replete detective returned with the lunch of the raging lawyer. From half-past three till four they prowled gently about the wood; at four they returned to the garden and sat on a bench in the garden, confident that their quarry must very soon return for food.

At four o'clock a flaming Eglantine came out of the house and accused them furiously of having murdered Lady Marion Ricksborough in the wood. It took them nearly twenty minutes to persuade her that they had not. They found it hard work; and doubted even then that they had wholly succeeded.

At half-past four Pollyooly said good-bye to the regretful Edward at the end of the High Street, whither he had accompanied her. She did not hurry up the hill, but as she went picked flowers to adorn the Honourable John Ruffin's chambers. When she did come into the garden, her eyes fell at once on the lawyer and the detective. They slept on the bench. The lawyer's head rested affably on the detective's shoulder. He looked not only redder but thinner, as if his quest in the warm wood had shrunk him a little.

Pollyooly did not awaken them; she went quietly into the house, and was welcomed by Eglantine with kisses and reproaches for the fright she had given her by her delay. Though in the end persuaded that she had not been murdered by the lawyer and the detective, she had begun to fear lest she were lost in the wood. She received Pollyooly's account of the pleasant day she had spent with many expressions of pleased amazement; and then she gave her a noble tea.

Pollyooly was coming to the end of it, listening with an agreeable show of interest to the further details of Eglantine's affair of the heart with the landed proprietor of the market-garden, when they were both startled by a loud snort at the window. The lawyer and the detective were looking in upon them, their faces beaming with satisfaction at the sight of their quarry. The detective guarded the window while the lawyer sprang lithely round the house, through the front door, and into the room.

"Thank goodness! I've caught your ladyship at last!" he cried.

Pollyooly scowled at him and said nothing. It was her habit in the part of Lady Marion Ricksborough to give herself airs. He snatched his watch from his pocket and cried:

"Oh, hang it! We've missed the last train to London!"

Pollyooly smiled coldly.

"Well, we must spend the night at the hotel," he said grumpily. "If I left your ladyship here, there's no saying when I should see you again."

Pollyooly scowled again, and Eglantine burst into loud and excited protest:

"Her ladyship must sleep in the house—in her own bed—properly."

The lawyer paid no heed to her protest, but bade her pack her young mistress's clothes at once. He said that the sooner she was at the hotel, the safer he would feel. He did not get his way without further and louder protests from Eglantine; but in the end he got it. She packed the little kit-bag for Pollyooly with clothes of Lady Marion. The detective carried it. As they were starting she gave Pollyooly two sovereigns wrapped up in a five-pound note, saying that the duchess had left it for her. The extra two sovereigns were for expenses, since she might need money to escape.

The sum warmed Pollyooly's heart.

She bade Eglantine an affectionate farewell and invited her to come to see her whenever she was in London. Then she set out with her captors. On the way down the hill the lawyer was very respectful and agreeable to Pollyooly, proclaiming his eager desire to secure her welfare, and dwelling on the pleasure she must be feeling at the prospect of being re-united with her affectionate father, the duke. No such prospect lay before her; and she displayed no interest in the matter. But when the lawyer, with a fatherly solicitude of his own, suggested that it would be safer if he took care of her money for her, she rejected the proposal with an uncommon, haughty curtness. He seemed somewhat hurt, but he did not press the matter. The detective addressed him as Mr. Wilkinson.

Pollyooly was not pleased to leave the pleasant and comfortable house of the duchess and its so noble breakfasts and teas, though it was some consolation that she was moving from it to an hotel where, in her ignorance of provincial England, she supposed that she would fare luxuriously. She was much less pleased to exchange the society of the lively Eglantine, so full of interesting confidences, for that of the ponderous and doubtless uncommunicative Mr. Wilkinson.

He was fully alive to his importance as being in charge of the daughter of a duke, and did not dream for a moment of putting her into the care of the detective. Indeed, in spite of his greater experience in taking charge of people, that worthy fellow was far too sleepy to be trusted with so elusive a child.

Mr. Wilkinson was far more affable and urbane with her than any one whom Pollyooly had ever met. He was careful to ask her whether she disliked the smell of tobacco smoke before taking her into the smoking-room, where he made a light meal on whiskey and soda and biscuits. He invited her to share his biscuits; but the noble tea was so recent that she was forced to decline.

As soon as he had finished it he accepted, with the readiest urbanity, her suggestion that they should go out on the sea-front. It was exceedingly gratifying to him to be seen walking hand in hand with the daughter of a duke. But his hand was hot and moist, and at the end of fifty yards of it Pollyooly withdrew hers from it with considerable decision.

"I'm not going to run away—to-day," she said firmly, putting it behind her back.

Mr. Wilkinson protested feebly; but since there seemed no likelihood of his recovering the hand, in the end he accepted the situation, saying pompously:

"I accept your ladyship's assurance that you will not try to escape."

"Not to-day," said Pollyooly haughtily; and she looked at him darkly.

"Oh, to-morrow you will be with his grace, and my responsibility ends," said Mr. Wilkinson in a tone of some satisfaction.

Pollyooly did not think that she would be with his grace on the morrow; but she did not say so.

Presently they sat down on a seat; and under the influence of the slight meal of which he had recently partaken, Mr. Wilkinson grew drowsily eloquent about the inestimable privilege she was about to enjoy of once more sharing her father's ducal home. But since the duke was not her father, and she had no intention whatever of sharing his ducal home, again the subject did not really interest her.

They returned to the hotel to dine; and since, while she was preparing for it, Mr. Wilkinson informed the manager of what he believed to be her rank and romantic history, during the meal she enjoyed a fine sense of self-importance, as the other guests stared at her—frequently with their mouths full.

Their interest compelled her to exercise her best manners; that she did not mind; but she did mind wasting the beautiful evening over a long dinner of no interest to her. In view of the fact that she had so lately eaten that noble tea, the earlier courses could hardly be expected to interest her; but the sweets to which she had been looking forward proved of a most disappointing, though painstaking, insipidity; and she was indeed glad when the meal came to an end.

Mr. Wilkinson talked affably, though with a touch of condescension not unnatural in one in charge of the daughter of a duke, to a colonel and golfer from Scotland, about the political situation. Pollyooly did not realise how much their deference to his opinions, drawn from that morning's *Daily Mail*, which both of them had read, was due to her presence beside him. After dinner they returned to the bench on the esplanade; and Pollyooly, for the first time in her life, had the opportunity of learning how sentimental, after a bottle of champagne, a middle-aged man can become about the moon. She gathered that he was deeply attached to a lady named Myra.

At half-past nine they returned to the hotel; and when she went to bed Mr. Wilkinson thoughtfully locked her in.

She slept well and rose early. The sea, smiling in the morning sun, attracted her greatly; and it seemed good to her to bathe. In view of the rank she was enjoying, it also seemed to her that she might very well have her way in the matter. She dressed quickly, and with the heel of her own stout shoe, a stouter shoe than Lady Marion ever wore, she began to hammer on her bedroom door.

She had not hammered long before an eager, respectful chambermaid came and asked her what she wanted. When she learned she hurried off to Mr. Wilkinson and awoke him. Mr. Wilkinson, desiring to sleep yet another hour, would not hear of any bathing. On learning this, Pollyooly hammered on the door yet more loudly than before with the heels of her two stout shoes. The chambermaid summoned the manager; both of them betook themselves to Mr. Wilkinson, and anxiously informed him that her young ladyship was awaking the whole hotel. Mr. Wilkinson, as angry as he could be with the daughter of so distinguished a client, was on the point of rising, when he had a happy thought. He bade the manager rouse the detective and tell him to take her young ladyship to bathe, and to look after her very carefully indeed.

The detective, also desiring to sleep yet another hour, rose gloomily and gloomily escorted Pollyooly to the sea. His gloom did not at all lessen Pollyooly's enjoyment of her bath and she spent the pleasantest half-hour in the sea. She graciously suffered the detective to pay for it.

She returned to the hotel with a glorious appetite and made a glorious breakfast. Mr. Wilkinson congratulated her on the healthiness of her appetite, with a somewhat envious air. It seemed to her that the hotel was more attractive in the matter of breakfasts than of dinners.

At a few minutes to eleven they started to walk to the station. Remembering that her parole only covered the day before, Mr. Wilkinson set her between himself and the detective. Pollyooly had not forgotten the Honourable John Ruffin's urgent instruction that she should wire him the time of the arrival of their train at Waterloo, and she learned from Mr. Wilkinson that it was three twenty-five. When, therefore, they reached the post office, she made a sudden dash across the road into it.

Mr. Wilkinson and the detective bustled after her and found her writing the telegram. It ran:

I arrive at three twenty-five. Pollyooly.

It puzzled them a little; and Mr. Wilkinson said:

"Why do you telegraph to Mr. Ruffin?"

"Because he told me to," said Pollyooly.

"He told you to?" said Mr. Wilkinson with a puzzled air. "When did he tell you to?"

"The day before yesterday," said Pollyooly.

Mr. Wilkinson shook his head with a pained air. He thought that her ladyship was fibbing.

"Why do you sign it 'Pollyooly'?" he said.

"Because it's my name," said Pollyooly.

Mr. Wilkinson shook his head with a yet sadder air. Had she been the daughter of a commoner, he would not have let her send the telegram; as it was he did. Half-way to the station he had grown yet more curious about it; and he asked her again why she had sent it.

"You'll know all about it when we get to London," said Pollyooly coldly.

He could get no more from her.

They lunched on the train, and under the expanding influence of a small bottle of champagne, the air of Mr. Wilkinson grew more and more triumphant at the success of his difficult mission.

When they descended from the train he clasped Pollyooly's right hand firmly, the detective clasped her left, and they walked down the platform. They had not gone thirty yards when they met the Honourable John Ruffin smiling agreeably.

"Hullo, Wilkinson! How are you?" he said cheerfully.

"How are you, Mr. Ruffin? At last we've found her little ladyship, and we're taking her to his grace. He will be pleased," said Mr. Wilkinson in tones of ringing triumph.

"Will he? Where is she?" said the Honourable John Ruffin with an air of lively curiosity.

"Here," said Mr. Wilkinson, drawing Pollyooly forward.

"Where?" said the Honourable John Ruffin, looking at Pollyooly with a somewhat puzzled air.

"Here!" said Mr. Wilkinson a little louder.

"Oh—*there*?" said the Honourable John Ruffin. "How are you, Pollyooly? I hope you had a pleasant time with Eglantine. But why have you come back so soon? I didn't expect you for some days."

"It was Mr. Wilkinson. He made me. He almost dragged me to his hotel," said Pollyooly.

"Oh, come, Wilkinson: this won't do, you know. This is kidnapping, you know—high-handed kidnapping," said the Honourable John Ruffin indignantly. "What do you think you're doing?"

"I'm taking her to the duke," said Mr. Wilkinson.

"And do you suppose that Osterley will be pleased at your

bringing him my housekeeper, Wilkinson? On the last occasion, when he did the kidnapping and took her home himself, he seemed very far from pleased."

The puzzled look had shifted from the Honourable John Ruffin's face to that of Mr. Wilkinson, and he said sharply:

"What do you mean?"

"I mean what I say," said the Honourable John Ruffin firmly. "I find you dragging my housekeeper, Mary Bride, along the platform of Waterloo Station, by main force, and with the help of a tall, strong man."

"I don't know what you are talking about!" cried Mr. Wilkinson stormily. "And if you'll forgive my saying so, I haven't any time to waste on your jokes, Mr. Ruffin!"

"Joke? Do you want me to show you how much of a joke it is by giving you in charge here and now for kidnapping my housekeeper, Mary Bride?" said the Honourable John Ruffin coldly.

Mr. Wilkinson's expression grew yet more puzzled and doubtful, and he said:

"Mary Bride? Who is Mary Bride?"

"Now what's the good of a subterfuge of this kind when you're holding her by the hand, Wilkinson? You should keep such tricks for maiden ladies!" cried the Honourable John Ruffin with a fine show of indignation.

"This is Lady Marion Ricksborough!" cried Wilkinson; but his tone lacked conviction.

Edgar Jepson

"It isn't. It's my housekeeper, Mary Bride. I wonder that a man of your knowledge of the world did not see at once that you were kidnapping the wrong person," said the Honourable John Ruffin; and *his* tone was full of conviction.

"I'm not Lady Marion, and I never said I was. It was you who said so. I am Mr. Ruffin's housekeeper, Mary Bride," said Pollyooly very firmly.

"B-b-b-but I've been c-c-c-calling her Lady Marion all the t-t-t-time, and she never p-p-p-protested once!" cried Mr. Wilkinson, gazing wildly at Pollyooly.

"Then all I can say is, you must have frightened the life out of her," said the Honourable John Ruffin indignantly. "And it will look bad—devilish bad—a man of your age kidnapping a child of twelve and frightening her to such an extent that she was afraid to tell you who she really was. Look here, am I to give you in charge here and now, and thresh the matter out in a police court? That will please Osterley!"

"Hold on a bit—hold on a bit," said Mr. Wilkinson faintly. "You're really not joking?"

"Certainly not," said the Honourable John Ruffin.

"Let's go into a waiting-room and talk it over quietly. We don't want to make any silly mistakes," said Mr. Wilkinson yet more faintly.

"I should think you didn't! You've made enough already," said the Honourable John Ruffin frankly. "But you'd better come along to my chambers. I've got Mary Bride's little brother there and a woman who has known her all her life. If you can't take my word for it, she'll convince you all right."

Mr. Wilkinson was very limp in the taxicab: he perceived that he had allowed his enthusiasm to carry him away with the result that he had been hopelessly duped. It was indeed mortifying, the more mortifying that he could not blame any one but himself—himself and nature. The more carefully he examined Pollyooly the more impressed he was by her likeness to Lady Marion Ricksborough. The detective was gloomy; he had lost a night's rest for nothing, as well as his hope of forthwith receiving the reward for the capture of the missing child, for it was he who had tracked her to the house in Devon. Now he might be months recovering her trail.

The Honourable John Ruffin on the other hand was in excellent spirits. He had no desire to embroil himself with his cousin, by definitely taking the side of the duchess in their quarrel; and he began to see plainly that the matter would never come to the duke's ears. Neither the lawyer nor the detective would talk about it; they both cut too ridiculous a figure.

At 75 the King's Bench Walk, they found Mrs. Brown and the Lump. Mr. Wilkinson needed no more evidence than the warmth with which Pollyooly kissed and hugged her little brother; but none the less he received Mrs. Brown's convincing assurances that she was Mary Bride.

When that worthy woman had been dismissed to the kitchen, he said heavily:

"This has been an unfortunate mistake—very unfortunate."

"Not so unfortunate as it would have been if Pollyooly had been ten years older. It would have cost you hundreds. As it is, I shouldn't wonder if she would be content with a fiver as compensation," said the Honourable John Ruffin with a soothing smile.

Mr. Wilkinson groaned; then he said:

"Well, I've made a mistake, and I suppose I must pay for it."

Slowly and sadly he drew a five-pound note from his notebook and handed it to Pollyooly.

"Thank you, sir," said Pollyooly; and dropped a curtsey, like the well-mannered child she was.

"Your housekeeper? To think that she should have roused the whole hotel to get that bath!" said Mr. Wilkinson bitterly.

"She was for the time being the daughter of a duke—by your appointment," said the Honourable John Ruffin suavely.

Mr. Wilkinson waved the detective out of the room, and followed him. At the door he paused to say very heavily:

"I shall never trust my eyes again."

"No: I shouldn't," said the Honourable John Ruffin gently. "I think another time, if I were you, I should try glasses."

CHAPTER VII

POLLYOOLY PLAYS THE GOOD SAMARITAN

Mr. Wilkinson had departed, a sadder but very little wiser man, and taken his detective with him; Mrs. Brown had been thanked, paid, and dismissed; and Pollyooly, having sufficiently fondled and kissed the irresponsive but unresisting Lump, went into the kitchen and set about getting ready the Honourable John Ruffin's tea.

She had lighted the gas under the kettle and taken the bread and butter from the cupboard, when he came into the kitchen, wearing an air of the most earnest purpose, and said impressively:

"Genius, Pollyooly—genius is the art of taking infinite pains."

"Yes, sir," said Pollyooly politely.

"That is why you are unsurpassed in the art of grilling bacon; you take infinite pains with it," he went on with the same earnestness.

"Yes, sir," said Pollyooly with more understanding.

"And now I am going to instruct you in the art of making tea," he said proudly. "I only learned yesterday that it was an art. Till then I believed that you merely poured boiling water on tea, and there you were. I have learned that it is not so. Also I have learned that that vegetable which comes from India and Ceylon, and is called tea by those who sell it, is not really tea at all. Tea only comes from China; and I have bought some."

"Yes, sir," said Pollyooly with the air of one receiving information gratefully.

"And now I will teach you the art of making it exactly as it was taught to me," he said with a very schoolmasterly air.

Thereupon, under his instructions, Pollyooly warmed the teapot and stood by the tea-caddy ready to put in two teaspoonfuls of tea (one for him, one for the pot) the moment the kettle boiled. The moment it did boil, following his instructions, she put the tea into the pot, and then, tilting the kettle without taking it from the stove, she poured the still boiling water on to it. Then she inverted the little glass egg-boiler and stood ready to bring the infusing tea into his sitting-room as soon as the upper half of it was nearly empty of sand.

Then he said in raised and sonorous tones of profound satisfaction:

"That is the art of making tea. Now that you have once learnt it, I know,—I am sure that very soon you will be not only the finest griller of bacon in England, but also the finest maker of tea."

"I'll try, sir," said Pollyooly cheerfully. "It doesn't seem very difficult."

"To genius nothing is *very* difficult," said the Honourable John Ruffin impressively. "The difficulty is to stick to it—to go on getting the thing right every time. But you can do it with bacon: why not with tea?"

When the sand had nearly all run out of the upper part of the glass, she took the tray into the sitting-room; he poured out a cup of tea, and declared that it was tea fit for the gods.

Pollyooly smiled at his satisfaction, and then said:

"Please, sir: I should like a note to Madame Correlli to say that I couldn't go to my dancing yesterday because I had to go into the country. She is so particular."

"Certainly; I will write it after tea," said the Honourable John Ruffin amiably.

After he had finished his tea he wrote the note and gave it to her. Then she paid a proud visit to the Post Office Savings Bank and added to her fattening account the sum of twelve pounds. Undoubtedly the Osterley family were valuable acquaintances.

Fortified by the exculpatory note from the Honourable John Ruffin, Pollyooly went next morning to her dancing class with an easy mind.

It had been clear to her friends that the career of house-keeper, admirably as she discharged its duties, was far inferior to her abilities; it did not give them nearly full scope. Those friends were young, and they were alive, keenly alive, to the fact that there is a steady demand for angels in that sphere of British and German industry curiously known as musical comedy. They could not conceive that, since she had to work for a living, Pollyooly's natural grace and the agility she had acquired in her earlier childhood, at the village of Muttle Deeping, and still retained, could be put to more agreeable and profitable use than that of helping to supply this demand for angels, and so help to raise the British ideal of womanly beauty.

For three mornings in the week therefore, Pollyooly, taking the Lump with her, went to Madame Correlli's dancing class in Soho; and thanks to her active early life at Muttle Deeping, was esteemed by that accomplished lady one of her most promising pupils. It is no wonder that Pollyooly and her young friend and fiance Lord Ronald Ricksborough, the heir of the Duke of Osterley, looked forward with confidence to the day when she should be a shining light of musical comedy and the proper wife for a British nobleman.

Madame Correlli read the Honourable John Ruffin's note with indulgence, accepted the excuse, and set Pollyooly to work.

Pollyooly was disinclined to make friends, close friends, of the other little girls in her class. She was indeed very civil to them, like the well-mannered child she was; but they did not greatly attract her. Belonging to hard-working, dancing families, they talked a great deal in their high-pitched, twanging voices about their friends and relations who danced at the Varolium, Panjandrum, and other music halls, friends of whom, since she herself aspired to higher things, Pollyooly had but a poor opinion. Moreover, many of them powdered their little faces, penciled their eyebrows, and deepened the roses in their cheeks with rose-carmine or rouge; and to Pollyooly, a daughter of Muttle Deeping, these practices were repugnant.

But she had formed one friendship among them, a friendship born of her protective instinct, with Millicent Saunders, a frail, pale wisp of a child, whose black eyes looked very big indeed in her thin face, framed in a mass of black hair. The other pupils were apt to look down on Millicent, because, though few of them ran to finery, Millicent was shabby indeed. Pollyooly was quite unaffected by this, for in the days when she had lived in the dreadful fear that she and the Lump might be driven by necessity into the workhouse, she had gone shabby herself. She knew that Millicent's mother, who had once been a dancer, was now a charwoman, often out of work, and in feeble health. It was Millicent's perpetual complaint that she herself was so slow growing up to the age at which she would be earning money and supporting her ailing mother. Down the vista of the future she saw a splendid vision in which her mother should always have a bloater with her tea. To Pollyooly Millicent always looked hungry.

It was Millicent's great pleasure to sit with the Lump on her knee in the intervals of their work, mothering him as long as he would suffer it; and it was her privilege to take his left hand as Pollyooly led him from Soho, across the dangerous crossings to the safe stretch of the embankment from Charing-Cross to the Temple. As they went Pollyooly and Millicent talked of the price of provisions and the trials of housekeeping.

But for the whole week before Pollyooly's trip to Devon Millicent had not been to the class. Pollyooly enquired and Madame Correlli enquired the reason for her absence, but none of the other pupils could tell them. It was now ten days since Pollyooly had seen her, and she was feeling anxious indeed about her.

Then, after the class was over, as she was leading the Lump down St. Martin's Lane on their way to the embankment he projected an arm and broke his placid and perpetual silence with one of his rare, but pregnant grunts. Pollyooly looked where he pointed, saw Millicent on the island in the middle of the roadway, and called to her.

Millicent turned her head and looked at them with somewhat dazed eyes. Her face did not as usual light up at the sight of the Lump. She crossed the road to them feebly.

"How are you? Why haven't you come to the classes for so long?" said Pollyooly.

"Mother's dead," said Millicent dully; and her big eyes which had been so dull, shone suddenly bright with tears.

"Oh, I'm so sorry!" said Pollyooly pitifully; and as she gazed anxiously at Millicent's seared and miserable face, her eyes grew moist with tears of sympathy.

Millicent stooped and kissed the Lump listlessly, almost mechanically.

"And what are you going to do?" said Pollyooly with grave anxiety.

She understood fully the seriousness of Millicent's plight.

"I'm going to the workhouse," said Millicent dully.

Pollyooly clutched her arm. It was impossible for her to turn pale for she was always of a clear, camelia-like pallor; but that pallor grew a little dead as she cried in a tone of horror:

"Oh, no! You can't go to the workhouse! You mustn't!"

Millicent looked at her with the lack-lustre eyes of the vanquished, and said in the same dull, toneless voice:

"I've got to. There's nowhere else for me to go to."

The tears in Pollyooly's eyes brimmed over in her dismay and horror at this dreadful fate of her friend; and she, the dauntless, Spartan heroine of a hundred fights with the small boys of Alsatia, was fairly crying.

"You mustn't go! You mustn't!" she cried.

"I didn't want to. I was trying not to," said Millicent slowly. "After mother's funeral yesterday Mrs. Baker, that's our landlady, said the relieving officer was coming round this morning to take me to the workhouse; and I ran away."

"Yes: that was the right thing to do," said Pollyooly in firm approval.

"Yes: I got up very early—just when it was light," said Millicent; and her voice grew a little firmer. "And I packed my clothes"—she gave the little bundle she was carrying a shake—"and then I sneaked down-stairs and out of the house. And oh, the trouble the front door gave me! You wouldn't believe! First it wouldn't open; and then when it did, it made noise enough to wake the whole house."

Pollyooly nodded with an air of ripe experience.

"I made sure they'd wake up and catch me and stop me. But they didn't; and I got out and ran hard out of the street. Then I walked about and then I sat on the embankment trying to think what to do and where to go. And two coppers wanted to know what I was doing all alone on my own."

"They would," said Pollyooly in a tone of deep hostility to the police force of London.

"Well, I said I was going to my aunt in Southwark. I had an aunt in Southwark once—only she's dead. But I couldn't think of anywhere to go—there didn't seem to be anywhere. So I thought I'd better go back to Mrs. Baker's and let them take me to the workhouse. At any rate she'll give me something to eat."

Pollyooly's tears had dried as she listened to her friend's tale; she wore an alert and able air which went but ill with her delicate beauty. She said quickly:

"Haven't you had anything to eat either?"

Millicent shook her head and said somewhat faintly:

"Not since supper last night. And I didn't eat much then—I wasn't hungry—not after the funeral."

"You wouldn't be," said Pollyooly sympathetically.

"And I hadn't any money. The funeral took all the money," Millicent added.

"Then the first thing to do is to get a bun," said Pollyooly in a tone of relief at seeing her way to do something. "Then you can come and have dinner with us."

"Thank you," said Millicent.

Her lips worked, as a hungry child's will, at the thought of food; and a faint colour came into her white cheeks.

Pollyooly started across the road with the Lump, and Millicent took his other hand.

On the other side of the road Pollyooly said firmly:

"You can't go to the workhouse. You mustn't. But we'll wait till we get home before we talk about that. But there must be some way for you not to go to it. We didn't."

They led the Lump down to the Strand; and at the first confectioner's shop Pollyooly bought Millicent a bun. The hungry child ate the first two mouthfuls ravenously; then she paused to break off a piece and give it to the Lump.

"No, no!" said Pollyooly quickly. "You eat it all yourself. You want it. He'll have his dinner as soon as he gets home."

"Oh, let me give him just a little piece," said Millicent.

"No: you're to eat it all," said Pollyooly firmly.

Most children of three would have burst into a roar on hearing this cruel prohibition. The placidity of the Lump was proof even against so severe a blow. He merely went on his way with a saddened air. Millicent ate the rest of the bun with eager thankfulness, brightening a little as the food heartened her.

They went down Villiers Street to the safe stretch of the embankment; and then Pollyooly, her brow knitted in a thoughtful frown, began to talk of Millicent's plight. The workhouse was so burning a subject that she could not wait to discuss it at home.

"You can't go to the workhouse; you can't really," she said. "If you could stay with us for a little while, you might find something to do. But it's for Mr. Ruffin to say whether you can stay with us. We live in his chambers, you know. I'm his housekeeper."

"Oh, if I could!" said Millicent wistfully.

"He might let you. He's very kind," said Pollyooly hopefully. "And if he did, I wonder what kind of a job you could get. What kind of work can you do?"

"I can do housework," said Millicent eagerly. "I always did our room—all of it. And I cooked all our meals. Mother went out such a lot, you know."

"It's something," said Pollyooly soberly. "But I expect you've got a lot to learn. You see I learnt a lot at Muttle Deeping. Aunt Hannah had a whole house there—before she lost all her savings in a gold mine and came to London. And she had everything like the gentry have—pictures, and plate, and brass candle-sticks—only not so much of them; and I learnt to clean them all. But I expect you'd learn too quickly enough."

"I'm sure I'd try," said Millicent.

"Yes. If Mr. Ruffin would let you stay for a week or two, I could teach you a lot," said Pollyooly hopefully.

For the rest of the way to the Temple they discussed in detail Millicent's accomplishments. They were few and limited; but to her willingness to work there were no bounds.

As soon as they reached the Temple they set about getting dinner. Fortunately Pollyooly had in her larder half a cold chicken; for, as was his practice, the Honourable John Ruffin had three days before ordered a cold chicken from the kitchen of the Inner Temple, had made a pretence of eating some of it at his breakfast, and then had bidden her never let him see it again. This was one of his ways of making sure that she and the Lump were properly fed, without weakening her independence by sapping her belief that she really supported the two of them.

Accordingly Millicent made an excellent meal; and it restored her strength and her spirits. She was surprised by the fact that the Lump had a whole mugful of milk with his dinner, for she was unused to this lavishness with that luxury in a child's diet. Pollyooly explained that it had been an article of faith with her Aunt Hannah that a young child needed a pint of milk a day; therefore the Lump always had one. Millicent was deeply impressed: this was indeed affluence.

She helped Pollyooly wash up after their dinner; and then Pollyooly suggested that it would be well for her to look very clean indeed when she was presented to Mr. Ruffin.

"He's so particular about children being clean. Mr. Gedge-Tomkins isn't nearly so particular," she said apologetically. "I work for him, too, you know. He lives across the landing."

Millicent accepted the suggestion readily enough, for her mother had been cleaner than her class. Pollyooly helped her wash and dry and brush out her mass of silken hair, and lent her a clean frock of her own. Presently, after the good meal on the top of her fast, Millicent turned very sleepy, and Pollyooly let her sleep. She was still sleeping when the Honourable John Ruffin returned home.

Pollyooly did not at once hurry to him with her news. She cut his bread and butter very thin and nice, and followed his instructions about the making of tea with scrupulous exactness. She carried the tray into his sitting-room and set it beside him. Then she hesitated, looking at him.

He looked up from the evening paper he was scanning, smiled his usual smile of appreciation at her angel face, and said amiably:

"Well, Mrs. Bride: what is it?"

When he did not call her Pollyooly he called her "Mrs." Bride, because they had decided that "Miss" Bride did not sound sufficiently dignified a name for a housekeeper.

"Please, sir: I've got a little girl here," said Pollyooly in a somewhat anxious, deprecating tone.

"A little girl?" said the Honourable John Ruffin in a natural surprise.

"Yes, sir. Her mother's dead; and they wanted to send her to the workhouse; but she ran away," said Pollyooly quickly.

"Curious that England's little ones should fly from the home she offers them," said the Honourable John Ruffin in his most amiable tone.

"Yes, sir. And she hadn't had anything to eat and she was very hungry, so I brought her home to dinner," said Pollyooly still quickly.

"A very proper thing to do," said the Honourable John Ruffin.

"And I thought I'd ask you if she could stop here, sir—with me and the Lump—till she gets some work to do. There'd be lots of room for her, sir; and she wouldn't bother you at all," said Pollyooly in a tone of anxious pleading.

"To get work might take a long time," said the Honourable John Ruffin gravely.

"Yes, sir; it might," said Pollyooly no less gravely, for she knew well the difficulty of getting work in London.

"And do you propose to keep her till she finds work?" said the Honourable John Ruffin in the tone of one who finds it difficult to believe his ears.

"Oh, yes, sir. She wouldn't eat much," said Pollyooly in a tone of cheerful serenity.

"Out of the exiguous wages Mr. Gedge-Tomkins and I pay you?"

"Yes, sir. I can do it quite well," said Pollyooly confidently; and then she added hopefully: "And perhaps it wouldn't be for long."

"On the other hand it may be for years and it may be forever," said the Honourable John Ruffin in a despondent tone.

"Oh, no, sir: I'm sure it wouldn't be as long as that," said Pollyooly confidently.

The Honourable John Ruffin looked at her earnest, anxious pleading face for half a minute. Then he said:

"Let's get it quite exact: you want to saddle yourself with the maintenance of a little girl for weeks, or it may be months, or even years, just to save her from the chief of England's representative institutions?"

Pollyooly's anxious frown grew deeper as she said:

"From the workhouse? Yes, sir."

> "Where shall the watchful sun,
> England, my England,
> Match the master-work you've done,

Edgar Jepson

England my own?"

quoted the Honourable John Ruffin with deep feeling. Then he added sententiously: "Well, we must by no means check the generous impulses of the young. But before I decide I should like to see your protegee. I take it that she does not rise to those heights of cleanliness at which you maintain yourself and the Lump; but does she display sufficient of our chief English virtue?"

"Oh, yes, sir: I couldn't have her about with the Lump if she wasn't," said Pollyooly firmly. "But I'll fetch her, sir." She paused, hesitatingly, and added: "She isn't in mourning, sir. The funeral took all the money."

"Then it can not be helped," said the Honourable John Ruffin sadly.

Pollyooly hurried up-stairs to Millicent, awoke her, and helped her tidy her hair. She bade her be sure and curtsey nicely to the Honourable John Ruffin, brought her into the sitting-room, and presented her to him. Millicent's big eyes were shining brightly from her sleep; her silken hair was prettily waved by its so recent washing; and the excitement of this fateful meeting had flushed delicately her pale cheeks. She appealed alike to the Honourable John Ruffin's aesthetic and protective instinct. Only her strong London accent distressed him: he feared lest it might corrupt the speech of Pollyooly and the Lump, which, owing to the care of their Aunt Hannah, who had for many years been housekeeper for Lady Constantia Deeping, was that of gentle-folk.

However, he talked kindly and sympathetically to Millicent, questioned her about her acquirements, and gave her leave to stay.

CHAPTER VIII

THE QUESTION OF A HOME

Millicent left his presence almost dazed with relief and joy. Not only was the imminent workhouse removed to a distance; but she herself was transported to a sphere of astonishing luxury. She settled down in a quiet content, only broken at rare intervals by a fit of weeping for her dead mother. She helped Pollyooly with the work of the two sets of chambers, displaying a considerable lack of knowledge and efficiency, and played untiringly with the Lump.

Between their dinner and the Honourable John Ruffin's tea she and Pollyooly hunted for work for her. Mr. Hilary Vance would have been an ideal, unexacting employer for her; but he was on the point of going to Paris for six months. They consulted all Pollyooly's friends; and all of them promised to look out for work for her; but it seemed likely to be hard to find.

The Honourable John Ruffin seeing Millicent often, watched and studied her carefully in the hope that his mind would produce a happy thought in the way of work for her. He perceived that she needed some well paid sinecure.

Then one morning when Pollyooly was clearing away his

breakfast, he said:

"I have been considering Millicent, and I should be charmed to let her stay here. You and she are such admirable foils to one another's fairness and darkness that no cultivated eye can rest on you together without great pleasure. But I don't think that you are doing the right thing in trying to find her a job like your own. She couldn't keep it. She is not a stern red Deeping like you. She is the clinging kind of orphan, not made to stand alone."

"But perhaps I should be able to go on helping her if she got work, sir," said Pollyooly, gazing at him with puckered brow. "I'm sure anybody would find her very willing."

"I'm sure they would. So many people are willing. Even the Government says it's willing. But I don't think that she is fitted to support herself by her own efforts yet. She has had no training; and evidently she hasn't been properly fed, and she isn't strong. What I think is that she's the kind of orphan for whom homes for orphans were created," he said with the air of one who has weighed the matter very carefully.

"Yes, sir," said Pollyooly in somewhat unhappy assent.

"At a home they would feed her up, give her open air exercise, and get her strong. Then they would train her to become the accomplished wife of one of our empire-builders in—er—er—in Canada, or British Columbia, or Rhodesia. And when she reached the marriageable age, they would export her and marry her to him. I think that that would suit her much better than being an independent, ill-paid worker in London."

Pollyooly considered his words carefully, frowning deeply. Then she said:

"Yes, sir: there's only herself. There isn't any one she wants living with her like I do the Lump. Perhaps a home would be better for her."

"I think it would," he said gravely. "You think it over."

Pollyooly told Millicent at once of his suggestion; and they discussed it seriously, and at great length. Indeed they talked of nothing else for the rest of the day. The more they talked of it the more they approved it. As Pollyooly said many times it was being settled in life for good—not like a job which you might lose; and always down the vista of the future, beyond the home, loomed the impressive and alluring figure of the marriageable empire-builder. They both came to the conclusion that the suggestion of the Honourable John Ruffin was indeed excellent.

Accordingly when she brought in his bacon next morning Pollyooly said:

"Please, sir: I think you're right about Millicent's going to a home; and so does she."

"Good," said the Honourable John Ruffin. "There can be no reasonable doubt that the mantle of Solomon, to say nothing of Benjamin Franklin's, has descended on your shoulders."

Pollyooly looked at him with the air of polite interest with which she was wont to receive his obscure sayings; then she said:

"Yes, sir. But how could she get into a home?"

"Oh, there are nominations and elections and that kind of thing," said the Honourable John Ruffin vaguely. "I'll find out all about it for you."

"Thank you, sir. I'll tell Millie."

Two days later he said to Pollyooly:

"I've been making enquiries about that home for orphans; and I've found a very good one. It's called the Bellingham Home. I had an idea that there was one in the family; and I find that my cousin and your acquaintance, the Duke of Osterley, is the president of it; and of course he can get an orphan into it in a brace of shakes. He only has to nominate her."

"Oh, that is nice, sir!" cried Pollyooly; and her eyes sparkled.

"Wait a bit," said the Honourable John Ruffin gloomily. "Unfortunately at the moment there is a coldness between me and the duke; and we may not warm to one another for months—not, in fact, till he wants me to do something for him. In these circumstances if I were to present an orphan to his attention he would be much more likely to wring her neck than nominate her."

"That is a pity, sir," said Pollyooly, and her face fell.

"Of course there are ladies of my acquaintance who dabble in charity; but they're not in the position of the duke. It would take them weeks to get Millicent into the Bellingham Home, while, if he nominated her, she would be dragged into it at full speed. She wouldn't be given time to breathe."

Pollyooly frowned in earnest consideration of the matter; then she said:

"Couldn't you ask a lady to ask him, sir?"

"It would be difficult to persuade one," said the Honourable

John Ruffin doubtfully. "You see, the duke has the reputation of being unamiable; and he has earned it well. My friends are only dabblers in charity; and I don't think they're keen enough on it to risk getting snubbed by him."

Pollyooly's thoughtful frown deepened as she cudgelled her small, but active, brain for a solution of this problem. Then she said:

"Perhaps if I was to go and ask him, he'd do it, sir."

"You?" said the Honourable John Ruffin very doubtfully. "I don't think that would do at all. You see there was that business of his kidnapping you in Piccadilly and carrying you off to Ricksborough House. He's not at all the kind of man to forget that he played the fool and had to pay you six pounds for doing it."

"But, please, sir, that wasn't my fault," said Pollyooly.

"No: it was his. That's why he's sure to be disliking you very much for it."

Pollyooly looked puzzled by this view of the working of the ducal mind.

"No: it wouldn't be any use at all," said the Honourable John Ruffin decisively.

For the while Pollyooly accepted his decision. But she accepted it with deep reluctance, for she was nearly as disappointed as Millicent by this dashing of their hopes. Naturally in that disappointment the Bellingham Home grew more and more attractive as it receded into the distance. She did not cease to discuss it with Millicent; and it grew clearer and clearer to her that it was worth her while to make the attempt to procure the duke's assistance in the scheme.

"He may be disagreeable. But he won't bite," she said in a somewhat contemptuous tone.

Accordingly a few mornings later she came to the Honourable John Ruffin with a very earnest face and said:

"Please, sir: I think after all I should like to go and ask the duke to put Millie into that home."

"You do?" said the Honourable John Ruffin in a tone of surprise. "Well, it's any odds that he'll refuse nastily."

"Yes, sir: but I think I ought to try. It would be so nice for Millie. Besides he won't bi—hurt me, sir," said Pollyooly firmly.

"No, he won't bite you. Dukes don't. Well, after all, if you don't mind being rebuffed, it is worth trying," said the Honourable John Ruffin.

"Yes, sir," said Pollyooly eagerly, very pleased to find that he did not forbid her outright to make the attempt.

The Honourable John Ruffin gazed at her thoughtfully; then he said in his best judicial tone:

"Well, if you're going to have a shot at it, there are one or two things you'd better do to give yourself the best chance of success. In the first place you must try to catch him after lunch, about a quarter to three—he's in a good temper then. And when you do catch him, don't be too gentle with him. Gentleness is rather wasted on Osterley. Be civil, of course, and be sure to address him as 'Your Grace' all the time. But be firm. Give yourself a few airs. After all, you are undoubtedly as much a red Deeping as Lady Marion; and Osterley's great grandfather was a Manchester tradesman."

"Yes, sir," said Pollyooly, and her eyes began to shine.

"And be sure to wear your prettiest frock," the Honourable John Ruffin went on. "I think your amber silk. Osterley, for all his cantankerousness, is as susceptible as the next duke."

"Oh, yes, sir: I'll wear my amber silk of course. And do you think I'd better take Millie with me so that he can actually see what she's like?"

The Honourable John Ruffin hesitated, pondering the question. Then he said with decision:

"No. Go alone. I think you'll be more effective alone. It will make Osterley feel more helpless."

"Very well, sir," said Pollyooly cheerfully.

During the morning she discussed with the excited and sympathetic Millicent the coming interview. She had the advantage of going to it in utter fearlessness. She knew the duke: he had been at Ricksborough Court during ten days of her stay there; and she had seen something of him every day. Also there had been the second and more violent meeting in Piccadilly when he had picked her up and carried her off to Ricksborough House under the firm conviction that she was his lost daughter. As a result of these two meetings Pollyooly had made up her mind that the duke was not a man to be feared by women. Millicent admired her fearlessness greatly.

After their dinner Pollyooly put on her amber costume, a silk frock, a pretty hat, stockings and gloves, all amber in colour and all matching, gifts of Hilary Vance. Regarding her thus attired, Millicent's great admiration became an even greater awe.

"Why, you look the perfect lydy," she said in a hushed voice.

"If I'm a red Deeping, I'm of the oldest blood in England, and I must be a lady. Mr. Ruffin says so," said Pollyooly in the tone of one quite sure of herself.

She charged Millicent to be very careful of the Lump, and to be sure to have the kettle boiling by four o'clock so that, should she be detained till then, she would have nothing to do on her return but forthwith make the tea. Then she sallied forth.

As she came into Fleet Street she met the Honourable John Ruffin.

"Ah: so you're off to the fray," he said; and his eyes warmed to the angel vision. "Well, you certainly have looks on your side; and that is three-quarters of the woman's battle. It's rather a score for you, too, that Osterley is one of the most susceptible dukes in England. But remember: don't be too civil to him; just bow. And then be firm—very firm."

"Yes, sir: I will," said Pollyooly very firmly indeed.

He stood considering her thoughtfully a moment; then he added:

"And I tell you what: if your prayers fail to move Osterley you might, as a last resort, try a few tears. Tears are dreadful things; and these cantankerous men can rarely stand them."

"Oh yes, sir: I will," said Pollyooly, her face growing bright with a look of perfect understanding.

He conducted her to her omnibus, put her on it, and wished her good luck.

Then he said after the bus had started:

"Don't forget the tears!"

He raised his voice in order to overcome the din of the traffic, and succeeded admirably.

CHAPTER IX

THE RELUCTANT DUKE

Tears were not at all to Pollyooly's liking. She considered them the sign of a feeble heart and softening brain. The Honourable John Ruffin had thrown quite a new light on them in suggesting that they could be used as a weapon; and she considered this use of them most of the way to Ricksborough House.

She reached it soon after half-past two. She found its gloomy nineteenth-century facade, black with the smuts of ninety years, a little daunting, and mounted its broad steps in some trepidation. But she rang the bell hard and knocked firmly.

Lucas, the butler of the duke, himself opened the door. At the sight of Pollyooly he started back; for the moment he thought that his lost young mistress stood before him.

Pollyooly stepped across the threshold, and said firmly:

"I want to see the Duke of Osterley, please."

The words showed Lucas his mistake; he perceived that before him stood not his mistress, but that young red Deeping who had once made a manifestly genuine offer to bite him; and he hesitated.

"It's very important. Please tell him that Miss Bride wants to see him," said Pollyooly.

"Um—er—come this way, miss. I'll see if his grace will see you," said Lucas in a doubtful voice.

He would have liked to refuse to let her into the house; but he was doubtful about her social standing. Therefore he took her to the nearest drawing-room, said that he would inform his grace, and betook himself to his master in the smoking-room, wearing a perturbed air, for the duke had as complete a vocabulary as any nobleman in England, and he might easily take it ill that this formidable red Deeping had not been refused admission to his house.

"If you please, your Grace, there's a young lady—leastways a little girl of the name of Bride—wants to see your Grace," said Lucas. "It's the little girl you brought home as turned out not to be Lady Marion."

"What the deuce did you let her in for?" said the duke on the instant; and he frowned at him.

"She said it was very important, your Grace," said Lucas in an unhappy tone.

The duke continued to frown, considering: Pollyooly might have brought word of his missing daughter; and he would by no means let slip an opportunity of getting information about her. On the other hand he might be about to be called upon to pay more for his kidnapping exploit. He had, however, just lunched ducally; and he was in a vainglorious mood, ready to face anything female.

At last he said bitterly:

"I seem to have every jackass in London in my service. Bring her here."

Lucas gloomily announced the readiness of the duke to receive her to Pollyooly. She followed him eagerly and came into the smoking-room with a brave air, though she was not feeling as brave as she looked. The duke stood on the hearthrug and glowered at her.

She did not hesitate; she gazed at his unamiable face with limpid eyes and said tranquilly:

"How do you do, your Grace?"

The duke grunted; then grew articulate, and said:

"What do you want?"

Pollyooly sat down deliberately in one of the big easy chairs facing him, and answered:

"If you please, your Grace, I came to see you about an orphan."

"An orphan?" said the duke a little less grumpily. He was somewhat impressed by the angel face of his visitor. During her last, compulsory visit it had been so much more red Deeping than angel. Also her costume so amber and so expensive impressed him.

"Yes: her name is Millicent Saunders; and they wanted to send her to the workhouse because her mother died who used to dance at the Varolium in the second row, but of course I couldn't let them do that, could I?" said Pollyooly in an explanatory tone.

"I don't know. What's it got to do with me?" said the duke quickly.

"Millicent is one of those orphans who wouldn't be much good working for herself, though of course she'd work hard and be very willing," said Pollyooly speaking very clearly in the explanatory tone, and looking at him with very earnest eyes.

"Then she'd better go to the workhouse. She'll have an idle enough time there," said the duke who was staunchly conservative in feeling.

"But she can't go to the workhouse," said Pollyooly in a deeply shocked tone.

"Why not?" said the duke.

Pollyooly looked at him very sternly, and said in a very stern voice:

"Her mother was a very respectable woman; she was in the second row of the Varolium ballet for years and years; and she always kept Millie very respectable. Besides, you can't let people go to the workhouse."

"Why can't you, if it's the proper place for them?" said the duke stubbornly, for he hated to hear the workhouse in any way disparaged, since he regarded it as a bulwark of society.

"How would you like your little girl to go to the workhouse?" said Pollyooly in a deeply reproachful tone.

"It's a prospect we needn't consider," said the duke haughtily.

"We never know what we may come to," said Pollyooly with a happy remembrance of the pious wisdom of her Aunt Hannah. "But Millie isn't going into the workhouse anyhow. I'm not going to let her. But she ought to go to a home and be trained to marry an empire-builder. She's that kind of orphan: Mr. Ruf—a gentleman says that she is. And I came to ask you if you'd give her a nomination so that she could go into the Bellingham Home. They'll do anything you tell them there; and if you said so, they'd take her in at once. And she'd be ever so much obliged to you. She'd never forget it—never. And so should I."

She was leaning forward with clasped hands and shining, imploring eyes. The duke was not insensible to the charm of her beauty, or to the appeal of her pleading voice. He was even more sensible to the tribute she had paid to his power in the matter of the Bellingham Home. But he was in a captious mood; and he did not wish to oblige her. His mind was chiefly full of the fact that he had made himself look foolish by kidnapping her and had had to pay her six pounds compensation. He was still sore about the foolishness and also about the money, for his was a thrifty soul.

But Pollyooly's angel face made a direct refusal difficult. He coughed and said:

"I—er—don't—er—do things in this—er—irregular way. My—er—nominations are—er—only given after I have been approached in the proper way and received testimonials and—er—sifted them out so as to nominate the most deserving orphan among the many applicants for admission."

"There couldn't be a more deserving orphan than Millie," said Pollyooly quickly.

"That remains to be proved. There are often fifty or sixty

applicants. And besides, this isn't the time of year when vacancies in the home are filled up," said the duke, hardening himself in his resistance, now that he could throw the odium of it on to the machinery of the home.

Pollyooly's face had fallen, for her instinct told her that he did not intend to grant her petition, and was only making excuses. She said slowly:

"But that wouldn't matter, because if you told them to take in Millie at any time of the year they'd do it."

"But the applications have to be written, setting forth the applicant's claims in the proper way," said the duke, falling yet more firmly back behind the safe barrier of red tape. "The matter has to receive careful consideration."

Pollyooly frowned thoughtfully: "Well, I could write. There are people who would tell me what to write," she said in the sad tone of one confronted with an uncongenial task. "Then you could consider Millie carefully. I'm sure you couldn't find an orphan who's more—more of an orphan than Millie."

"I'm afraid it wouldn't be any use—not at this time of year," said the duke almost cheerfully, as he saw that in an irreproachable fashion he was getting his own disobliging way.

Pollyooly filled with the bitter sense of defeat. She heaved a deep sigh and was on the point of rising to go, when the last adjuration of the Honourable John Ruffin flashed into her mind, and on the instant she grew eager to try the new weapon he had suggested. She looked at the duke with a calculating eye. Nature, thinking probably that if was enough for a man to be a duke, had not been lavish of beauty to him: his somewhat small features were often set in an unamiable expression, and with the faint light of evil satisfaction at baulking Pollyooly now on them, they looked more unamiable than usual. He did not indeed seem to be a man to be easily softened. But the matter was far too important for her to lose the only chance left.

Very deliberately she drew her handkerchief from her pocket, blinked her eyes hard to make them water, hid them under the handkerchief, sniffed once but loudly, and then sobbed.

"It's very—hard—on Millie—she'll be—dreadfully—disappointed!"

A sudden consternation smote the duke. He had looked to make himself completely disagreeable at his ease, certainly without any such assault on his feelings as this. He shuffled his feet and said hurriedly:

"It's no good crying about it. It can't be helped, you know."

Pollyooly's quick ear caught the change in his tone. She sobbed more loudly:

"Oh, yes—it can—you could do it—if you wanted to!"

"These things have to be done in the proper way," protested the duke.

"It isn't that. You—you—don't like Millie!" sobbed Pollyooly, watching the weakening face of the perturbed nobleman with an intent eye over the top of her handkerchief. "You—you—hate her!"

"Why, I've never set eyes on her!" cried the duke.

"Oh, yes: you do—and it's—it's beastly," sobbed Pollyooly.

No duke likes to hear his conduct described as beastly by an angel child—especially when the description happens to be accurate—and the duke ground his teeth.

Pollyooly, watching him, sobbed on—louder.

The duke gazed at her in a dismal discomfort. He shuffled his feet till the shuffle was almost a dance. Then he said in a feebly soothing tone:

"There—there—that'll do."

Pollyooly's sobs grew yet louder—heartrending.

The duke took a hurried turn up and down the room.

Pollyooly, a huddled figure of desperate woe, sobbed on.

The duke grabbed at his scrubby little moustache and held on to it firmly. It was no real help.

He ground his teeth; he tugged at his moustache; and then in a tone of the last exasperation, he cried:

"Oh, hang it all! Stop that infernal howling; and I'll give you the nomination!"

Pollyooly softened her sobs a little; the duke flung himself down into the chair before the writing-table, at the other end of the room, and seized pen and paper.

"What's the brat's name?" he growled.

"Millicent—Saunders," sobbed Pollyooly.

The duke wrote the nomination, put it in an envelope, addressed it to the secretary of the Bellingham Home, licked the flap of the envelope with wolfish ferocity, and banged it fast.

He came hastily across the room with it to Pollyooly, held it out, and said with even greater ferocity:

"Here you are—and—and—much good may it do her!"

Pollyooly rose quickly and took it. She could hardly believe her shining eyes.

"Oh, thank you, your Grace! Millicent will be so glad!" she cried joyfully.

The duke growled in his throat; but in some way Pollyooly's radiant angel face blunted his ferocity. Also it robbed his surrender of its sting. He rang the bell; then opened the smoking-room door for her and bade her good day quite in the manner and tone of an English gentleman.

On the threshold, like the well-mannered child she was, she paused to thank him again. When she went out he shut the door quite gently; and by the time he had settled down again in his easy chair, he was feeling truly magnanimous.

CHAPTER X

POLLYOOLY AND THE LUMP
GO TO THE SEASIDE

The motor-bus which carried Pollyooly home crawled, to her impatient fancy, no faster than the old horse-bus, so eager was she to pour the news of her success into the ears of Millicent.

Millicent, however, after her first joy on hearing that the path which would ultimately lead her to the altar with an empire-builder was open to her, grew sad.

"It's a pity I couldn't stay on and on with you here," she said very plaintively. "I'm sure I shall never be so happy anywhere else."

"Oh, yes: you will," said Pollyooly firmly. "You'll find the home ever so nice."

Millicent shook her head doubtfully and said:

"And I shan't see anything of you and the Lump any more."

"Oh, yes: you will. You let us know when visiting day is—there's sure to be a visiting day to a home; and we'll come and see you."

Millicent's face grew a little brighter.

The Honourable John Ruffin congratulated Pollyooly warmly on her success; then he said:

"I trust you were not driven to use the weapon I suggested. Osterley's cantankerousness didn't go so far as that?"

"Oh, well, sir," said Pollyooly, hesitating a little—"I—I did have to pretend to cry."

The Honourable John Ruffin laughed gently.

"Poor Osterley!" he said.

The duke's letter plainly stirred the Bellingham Home to instant activity, for a letter came for Pollyooly by the first post to say that an official of the home would come for Millicent that very afternoon.

During the morning Millicent wept several times at the thought of leaving the Lump; and her final farewell was tearful indeed. But Pollyooly believed that her sadness would not last long: they had decided that the empire-builder would have fair hair and a large and flowing moustache.

After Millicent's departure their life settled down into its usual even tenour. Pollyooly missed her; and doubtless the Lump also missed his devoted and obedient slave, though he was of too placid a nature to raise an outcry about his loss. She wrote to Pollyooly on the day after her arrival at the home; and the letter made it clear that her first impressions of it were pleasing.

It was on the fifth morning after her going that the Honourable John Ruffin made the great announcement. It was his habit to chant in his bath what Pollyooly believed to be poetry; and it is improbable that an observant child of twelve, who had passed the seven standards at Muttle Deeping school, could have been mistaken in a matter of that kind. At any rate his chanting was rhythmical. The habit may have borne witness to the goodness of his conscience, or it may not (it may merely have been a by-product of an excellent digestion), but that morning it seemed to her that he chanted more loudly and with a finer gusto than usual.

She was not greatly surprised therefore, when she brought in his carefully grilled bacon, at his saying in a very cheerful tone:

"I have had a windfall, Mrs. Bride—a windfall of thirty-five pounds. It fell out of an auction-bridge tree—a game you do not understand—and it has made the heat-wave, which ought to be called the heat-flood, more unbearable than ever. Therefore I have resolved to go away for a while to the sea."

"Yes, sir," said Pollyooly in a tone of amiable congratulation.

But her face fell a little; for though the departure of the Honourable John Ruffin meant that she would have less work; it also meant that she would have to spend more on food for herself and her little brother the Lump, since the Honourable John Ruffin did not eat all his bread or drink all his milk; and there was often half a cake with which he refused to continue his afternoon tea on the ground that it was stale. Besides, life was a far more cheerful business when he was at home; his talk was Pollyooly's chief diversion, though she was hardly conscious of the fact; and it frequently gave her to think deeply.

"But the thing that has kept me so long in London submerged in the heat-flood has not been so much the want of money (I have had enough for my own escape) as the great bacon difficulty," he said and paused.

"Yes, sir," said Pollyooly.

"But, thanks to this windfall, I can get over that difficulty by taking you to the sea to grill my bacon for me, and the Lump to keep you occupied while you are not grilling it, that Satan may not find some mischief still for idle hands to do," he said sententiously.

Pollyooly's large blue eyes opened very wide; and her mouth opened too.

"Oh, sir, me and the Lump, sir!" she said in a hushed, breathless voice of incredulous rapture.

"You and the Lump. The Lump and the sea were made for one another. I look to see him an admiral one of these days. It is time that England had a red-headed admiral; I'm tired of these refined, drab-haired ones. It is my patriotic duty to give him a taste for the sea early."

"Oh, thank you, sir!" said Pollyooly in a tone of profound gratitude.

"We will go to Pyechurch. There's an old family servant of ours who lets lodgings at Pyechurch. I made her life a burden to her when I was young; and consequently, with true womanliness, she has always entertained the strongest affection for me. It would be no use taking you to any other lodgings because you wouldn't be allowed to grill my bacon for me. But Mrs. Wilson knows that I must be humoured; and humoured I shall be. Also she will look after you while I am playing golf at Littlestone—not that I have ever known you to need looking after."

"Oh, sir, it will be nice!" said Pollyooly, still somewhat breathless.

The Honourable John Ruffin smiled at her amiably.

"This morning we will pack; this afternoon we will go," he said.

Pollyooly had to slip up to their attic at once to tell the Lump, who was playing there peacefully, the splendid news. He received it in placid silence; apparently it did not seem to him to be a matter on which he was called to comment either favourably or unfavourably. Pollyooly moved about the world on very light, dancing feet; and as soon as she had washed up the breakfast things she packed their small wardrobes in the brown tin box. Then the Honourable John Ruffin, having finished his cigar and *Morning Post*, summoned her to help him pack.

For a while she observed his fashion of doing so with pain and dismay. He put his clothes in the portmanteau anyhow and crushed them firmly down. Sometimes he stood on them, quietly.

Standing painfully now on one leg and now on the other, she endured the sight for several minutes; then she said:

"Oh please, sir: you'd better let me do it."

"Why? What's wrong with my way of doing it?" said the Honourable John Ruffin, looking down at the confused mess with some surprise.

"Look how you're crumpling your shirts, sir," said Pollyooly.

"I thought that that was what trunks and portmanteaux were for. But have it your own way. Deal with it yourself," said the Honourable John Ruffin with airy indifference.

He lighted another cigar and watched Pollyooly take the clothes out of the portmanteau and replace them neatly with some regard to their shape and the space to be filled, finding room for a dozen things which he had been forced to leave out. Then, when she had filled half the portmanteau, he said:

"Always fresh accomplishments, Mrs. Bride. If you go on at this rate, you will certainly go down to posterity as the Admirable Pollyooly."

He sent down to the Inner Temple kitchen for his lunch; and Pollyooly gave the Lump his dinner. She ate little herself; she was too excited. They drove, proudly, in a taxicab to Cannon Street Station; and they travelled, proudly, first-class.

The Honourable John Ruffin had bought picture papers for the two children and a novel for himself, and now and again he paused in his reading to observe them. It was always a pleasure to a man of his aesthetic sensibility to gaze at Pollyooly's angel face in its frame of beautiful red hair and at that redder-headed but authentic cherub, the Lump. As they ran through London, curiously curled round the Lump, she was busy showing him the pictures in the papers and receiving his monosyllabic comments on them, with the ecstatic delight with which his disciples receive, or should receive, the pregnant utterances of a genius. When they came into the country she was busy pointing out to him, with an even more excited delight the common railside objects. It was more than a year since he had been in the country; and he had to be told earnestly and more than once that a cow was a cow and a sheep a baa-lamb, for he was inclined to class them all alike under the genus gee-gee. When at last he did correctly hail a sheep as a baa-lamb, the triumphant pleasure of Pollyooly passed all bounds.

The Honourable John Ruffin read and observed the children, and observed the children and read. But when they were nearing their journey's end, he shut up his book and said:

"I think it will be well for you to cease to be my housekeeper at Pyechurch, Mrs. Bride. People will ask you about our relations of course, because by the sea there is so much time for idle curiosity; and you had better tell them that you are a cousin of mine. That is nothing but the truth, for you are undoubtedly a red Deeping; and all the Deepings, red or neutral-tinted, are cousins, first, second, third, fourth, and so on, of mine."

"Yes, sir," said Pollyooly gravely.

"Also I think that you had better give yourself a few airs. You will have a better time that way, for airs procure you a welcome in the best circles. Be a red Deeping—not too truculent, you know, but firm."

Pollyooly's eyes sparkled a little; and she said:

"Yes, sir: I should like to. I like being a red Deeping, sir, rather. I liked it when I was at Ricksborough Court."

"Good. You have the right spirit. One of these days you will become what the newspapers call a society leader. I foresee it," he said in a tone of the most assured conviction.

"Yes, sir," said Pollyooly.

Edgar Jepson

"There's one difficulty though, and that's your hands. At present they're hardly the hands of a red Deeping," he said thoughtfully. "Not that they're not small and well-shaped!" he interjected hastily. "But I expect that a week's idleness will let your nails grow; and brushing will do the rest."

"Yes, sir," said Pollyooly.

She had never considered her hands from the aesthetic standpoint. She had been content to keep them clean. She considered them now, ruefully. It is indeed hard to do the work of two sets of chambers in the Temple without the hands showing it. Her nails were very short and rather jagged; a thumbnail was broken; the skin about them was rough and broken. She looked from them to the white, carefully kept hands, with pink shining nails, of the Honourable John Ruffin, and sighed.

"I think that for the future you'd better work in gloves," he said in a sympathetic tone.

"I think I'd better try," said Pollyooly doubtfully. To her firm spirit the idea of working in gloves savoured of dilettantism.

"You see a lady—and all red Deepings are gentlefolk of course—a lady must have good hands," said the Honourable John Ruffin in a deprecating tone.

"Yes, sir," said Pollyooly solemnly.

It was the first time that the meaning of the fact that the Deeping blood ran in her veins had been brought home to her; and she flushed faintly with honourable pride at the thought that she was a lady, for all that she did the work of two sets of chambers in the Temple. She sat a little more upright.

"And there's another thing," he went on. "At Pyechurch I shall call you Pollyooly; and you will call me John, or cousin John."

"I—I'll try to remember, sir," said Pollyooly, again flushing with pride.

"You'll soon get into it," said the Honourable John Ruffin cheerfully. "And it will be very nice for me to have a cousin always to hand."

Pollyooly flushed again; and the gratitude in her eyes as they rested on him was beyond words.

The train, one of the South-Eastern best, sauntered leisurely through the pleasant, sunny landscape, stopping meditatively at stations and between stations, as the whim took it, but at last it reached Hythe.

They drove from there, proudly, in a wagonette to Pyechurch, along the edge of Romney Marsh, with the shining sea on their left hand. Pollyooly enjoyed the felicity of showing it to the Lump, who had never before seen it; but she was somewhat taken aback by his hailing a ship as a baa-lamb.

They found Mrs. Wilson eagerly awaiting them. There was no doubt of her affection for the Honourable John Ruffin. She had a sumptuous tea ready for them; and after the journey and its excitement they dealt with it heartily.

Any fear that the Honourable John Ruffin had felt of Mrs. Wilson's objecting to Pollyooly's grilling his bacon passed away when he saw how her heart went out to the two children. Indeed, before tea was over he was driven to say:

"I see what it is, Mrs. Wilson: the Lump is going to usurp my place in your regard."

"No one could do that, Master John; and well you know it," said Mrs. Wilson firmly.

CHAPTER XI

POLLYOOLY MEETS THE
UNPLEASANT PRINCE

Tea over, the Honourable John Ruffin proposed that he should take them to the sands; and Pollyooly agreed eagerly. But as they came out of the house, two little girls, bare-legged and wearing sandals, passed them.

He looked from them to Pollyooly's stout shoes and black stockings, stopped short and said firmly:

"We must change all this."

He turned to the right down the street and led them into the chief shop of the village. Apparently he was well known there, for the proprietor greeted him with respectful warmth. He bought sandals, bathing-dresses, blue linen frocks, a sunbonnet for Pollyooly, a linen hat for the Lump, spades and buckets.

Loaded with these purchases he came out into the street, and took his way back to Mrs. Wilson's, saying:

"You must hurry up and change into these things. First impressions are so important at the seaside; people have so much leisure to be pernickety in; and you *must* look all right!"

Pollyooly was not long making the change; and when she came out of the house in the blue linen frock and sunbonnet, he smiled at her with warm approval and said:

"There's no doubt about it, you have got the knack of wearing clothes, Pollyooly."

To Pollyooly his utterance was entirely cryptic; but she gathered that it was complimentary and returned his smile.

He took them down to the sands; and they were soon at the height of happiness, building a castle, paddling, and picking up shells. He left them to it; and went for a stroll down the sea wall. Since it was a hot evening, at seven he fetched them to bathe; and since he let them bathe in their own timid way, the timid way of children bathing for the first time, they enjoyed it exceedingly. The Lump found eight inches of water deep enough for him, Pollyooly eighteen.

The next morning they bathed again at seven.

The house was near enough to the sea to allow them to go straight from their bedrooms to it in their bathing dresses. After their bath the Honourable John Ruffin returned firmly to bed for an hour and so gave Pollyooly time to make a leisurely and complete breakfast before grilling his bacon. He had explained to Mrs. Wilson that it was necessary to his happiness that it should be grilled by Pollyooly, and she had raised no objection. She observed the process with interest, but not with approval.

"All that time spent over cooking a few slices of bacon!" she said with the womanly air of one sniffing, when it was transferred from the frying-pan to the dish.

Pollyooly's brow puckered in a thoughtful frown; and she said gravely:

"But that's the only way to get it right."

Mrs. Wilson sniffed outright.

After his breakfast the Honourable John Ruffin departed to Littlestone to golf; and Pollyooly and the Lump went down to the sands. There are no niggers, pierrots, or bands at Pyechurch, only a few donkeys and a cocoanut-shy. But at low tide there are a thousand acres of firm sand, a children's paradise. Pollyooly enjoyed it beyond words: not only the sands and the sea but also the freedom from care. Food, excellent food and plenty of it, awaited them, paid for, at Mrs. Wilson's.

The Lump was the cause of Pollyooly's first introduction to fellow-sojourners in this delectable land. A little girl of four, with very large brown eyes, who was playing near them, was quite suddenly attracted by him, and without further ado took possession of him. Pollyooly was pleased that he should have a playmate of his own age; the little girl's nurse, observing that they were dressed as other children and that Pollyooly spoke "prettily," and was inclined to be uncommonly haughty with her, assented to the acquaintance. The little brown-eyed girl's blue-eyed sister, Kathleen, who was seven, mothered her little sister, whose name was Mary. Also now and again she mothered the Lump; but Pollyooly was not jealous.

At first the Lump was somewhat taken aback by this sudden acquisition of a female friend; but his remarkable placidity stood him in good stead, and he endured it with an even mind. Presently indeed he seemed to be taking pleasure in it, for he began to bully her in the manliest fashion.

Then the mother of the little girls joined them and was at once charmed by the Lump. Pollyooly found no need to display the airs of a red Deeping, with which she had been treating the nurse, to her; and presently they were chatting in the friendliest way. Mrs. Gibson, as the nurse called her, seemed as taken with Pollyooly's serious outlook on life as with the charm of the Lump; and presently she asked her if her mother would let them come to tea with Kathleen and Mary and to games on the sands after it that afternoon.

Pollyooly explained that they were staying with their cousin John, who had gone to golf at Littlestone and would not be back till late; therefore she accepted the invitation herself. Mrs. Gibson was impressed by the discovery that cousin John was the Honourable John Ruffin; but she expressed her surprise that he should have gone away for the day and left them to themselves without a nurse to look after them. Pollyooly, with an air of considerable dignity, assured her that she would never dream of trusting the Lump to a nurse; and Mrs. Gibson admitted that she was right.

Pollyooly and the Lump enjoyed the party exceedingly. There were a dozen children, fellow-guests; and at tea the manners of the Lump, under Pollyooly's anxious eye, were beyond reproach. Her hands indeed troubled her, and she kept them out of sight as much as she could. After all they were not very large hands to withdraw from view. After tea the younger children played in the charge of nurses; the elder children, to the extreme delight of Pollyooly, who loved to run fleetly, disported themselves in more swift and violent games. She had much to tell the Honourable John Ruffin on his return from Littlestone. He congratulated her warmly on their debut.

The next day she found herself well launched in the society of the sands, with many playmates, and entered upon the fullest and most delightful life. But there is always a fly in the finer ointments; and the Pyechurch fly was Prince Adalbert of Lippe-Schweidnitz.

That morning Pollyooly had her first sight of him. She and the Lump were playing with Kathleen and Mary, when Kathleen cried in a tone of dismay, "Here's the prince!" picked up Mary, who would have gone quicker on her own feet, and staggered off toward their nurse with her.

Pollyooly picked up the Lump and came with her, though she could see no reason for Kathleen's dismay, for the prince was but a fat little boy of ten, small-eyed, thick-lipped, and snub-nosed. His white sailor suit seemed to give his ugliness its full values.

Under the wing of their nurse Kathleen and Mary surveyed him with the eyes of terror; and Kathleen poured into Pollyooly's attentive ear the story of his dreadful doings: how he had pushed a little boy over the edge of the sea-wall, kicked several others; how he had hit little girls with their own spades and pulled the hair of others; how he never passed a carefully built castle without kicking a breach in it, and always threw any spades or buckets he could lay hands on far into the sea.

Pollyooly observed this terror with the unimpressed eye of a connoisseur. When she had lived with her Aunt Hannah in the little slum at the back of the King's Bench Walk, she had fought many battles with the small boys of Alsatia; and she was not at all impressed by the physique of the prince. She was of the opinion that Henry Wiggins would make very short work of him; and she could hold Henry Wiggins (by the hair) with her left hand and smack him with her right till she was nearly as tired of smacking as he was of being smacked. She knew that she could because she had done it.

The prince came to the castle they themselves had been building and kicked down one wall of it.

"If only you weren't a prince, I'd teach you, my fine young gentleman," said the nurse softly.

"You mind the Lump! I'll go and smack him hard!" cried Pollyooly with eager confidence.

"No! No! He's a *prince*! You mustn't touch a *prince*, miss!" cried the nurse in a tone of the last horror, gripping Pollyooly's wrist tightly. "Besides, he'd hurt you. He's a very nasty, spiteful little boy."

"Oh, I don't mind him! I'm not afraid of a little boy like that!" cried Pollyooly; and she tugged at the restraining grip, hard but in vain, eying the pest with the bright light of battle in her eyes.

"I wouldn't let my children play with him like some people do just because he's a prince—not was it ever so. I should be frightened all the time," said the nurse.

"If he ever touches the Lump, I'll teach him!" Said Pollyooly with a cold, impressive ferocity.

"If ever he touches one of us, papa will spank him hard. Papa doesn't care much for princes," said Kathleen.

"I should think he didn't—if they're like that," said Pollyooly with conviction.

They watched the devastating royal progress with indignant eyes. The back view of the prince was nearly as unpleasant as the front, for he slouched along with his fat little figure hunched forward in a very ugly fashion. The children fled before him as he came, and from the shelter of their nurses, or their mothers, angrily watched him destroy the castles they had built. But most of their mothers regarded him with a gloating admiration; they felt that the beach was more glorious for his royal presence.

About forty yards behind him came a companion figure, his equerry the Baron von Habelschwert, a stout, pig-eyed, snub-nosed man of forty-five who walked with the stiffness of a ramrod of the best Bessemer steel. His legs were, unfortunately, rather short, and since the lower part of his body was of a fine protuberant rotundity which the breadth of his shoulders and the thickness of his chest failed dismally to equal, he displayed an uncommonly exact resemblance of a perambulating pear. He had a rich expanse of fat cheek and a small, but dimpled, chin. He was saved by his fierce moustache, which, upturned in the imperial fashion, gave him the ferocious air required by his military profession and his sentiments of a superman of the latest Prussian brand.

Happiness sat enthroned upon his brow. A passion for blacking is a distinguishing characteristic of his military caste; and his natural love of licking the boots of members of the many royal families of the Fatherland was finding its full expression. In Prince Adalbert he had a perpetual boot to lick. Sometimes indeed the boot licked him: that very morning the prince had kicked his shins in a masterly fashion, on being invited to wash his face for the day. The baron bore it very well.

His clothes fitted him with an extreme, but somewhat unfortunate, military tightness. They were of an unpleasant greenish tint which did not match the green Homberg hat he wore. In his right hand he carried a short cane and yellow gloves. The morning was hot; his boots were patent leather. Diffusing an agreeable odour of pomatum on the breeze, he walked with the air of one taking his ease in a conquered country, for he was one of the gallant German war-party, and he looked forward with touching certainty to the day when the mailed fist of his imperial master should sweep England with fire and sword from sea to sea. He often talked in a gloating fashion of that great day to his young charge. Possibly that was one of the reasons which induced Prince Adalbert of Lippe-Schweidnitz to make so free with the castles and persons of the children of the so-soon-to-be-subjugated English.

The ogres of the sands having disappeared down the beach, the children repaired the damage to their castles and once more played in peace. That afternoon there was another royal progress of the same devastating kind but more complete, since the prince surprised a little girl and pulled her hair. The fond English mothers still observed him with a gloating air, happy to be on the same stretch of sand with him. They said indulgently to one another: "Boys will be boys," or, with conviction: "Such a manly little fellow."

This time the Baron von Habelschwert walked only fifteen yards behind the prince. He smiled benignly on the destruction of the castles; plainly he felt that his young charge was treating the so-soon-to-be-subjugated English in the right spirit.

There was only one check to the royal progress. The sand-castle on which Pollyooly and Kathleen had worked so hard stood directly in the line of it. Kathleen and Mary fled to their nurse at the approach of the prince, calling wildly to Pollyooly to follow. Pollyooly leaving the Lump in the castle, stepped out of it, and spade in hand calmly awaited the coming of the prince.

When he was three yards from her she said quietly but very distinctly:

"You keep away."

The prince advanced two steps and stopped. There was that in Pollyooly's deep blue eyes which gave him pause. He advanced another step, and stopped again. Then he called her "pig-dog," in his native tongue, turned aside, and pursued his way. As he went he kept looking back at her, scowling malevolently.

Pollyooly gazed after him with unchanging face. She would have liked to put her tongue a long way out at him; but she felt that red Deepings did not do so.

The nurse came down to the castle with Kathleen and Mary, and said in a tone of respectful awe:

"However you dare, miss! And him a prince too!"

"I don't care a pin for him," said Pollyooly calmly.

She stepped back to the castle and continued the work of construction.

CHAPTER XII

WHAT THE PRINCE ASKED FOR

The royal progress was the event of the morning and after-noon for several days before it occurred to Pollyooly to tell the Honourable John Ruffin about it. Then one evening, on their way to bathe, she told him.

The Honourable John Ruffin stood still on the edge of the sea, looked at her thoughtfully, and said:

"This is interesting indeed. I had no idea that German aggression had extended to this retired spot."

"And he's such an ugly little boy," said Pollyooly.

"And he is all alone?"

"Oh, no: there's a baron with him to look after him—with a large moustache. He's very ugly too," said Pollyooly frankly.

"This grows more interesting still. I think I should enjoy looking into this matter. Prussian barons always need a firm hand. But I'm too full up with golf to deal with it for the next day or two. I must bear it in mind."

Plainly he did bear it in mind, for on the afternoon of the third day, to Pollyooly's delight, he joined them on the sands. She introduced him to Mrs. Gibson; and he thanked her for having had his two little cousins to tea, and chatted to her in his cheerful and engaging fashion till Prince Adalbert of Lippe-Schweidnitz came slouching along on his devastating course. The Honourable John Ruffin observed him with every appearance of the liveliest interest; but the Baron von Habelschwert seemed to afford him even greater pleasure than did his young charge; and upon him he gazed with a fascinated, loving eye.

"I have rarely seen a more perfect pair," he said to Mrs. Gibson in a tone of deep content.

"Detestable creatures!" said Mrs. Gibson with some heat.

"Perhaps—but how incomparably Prussian!" said the Honourable John Ruffin with warm appreciation. "And you let these unpleasant ones terrorise your children?"

"Well, what can I do?" said Mrs. Gibson. "My husband would have stopped it, if he had been down here; but he isn't. I have spoken to one or two men, acquaintances, about it. But they seem afraid to interfere."

"We are getting too highly civilised," said the Honourable John Ruffin in a melancholy tone. "The fine old English spirit is dying out; and they're afraid of getting into the papers. But evidently what is needed is the giving of lessons; and the proper person to give them is a fierce small boy— Irish for choice—one who is always and nobly spoiling for a fight. Unfortunately I have not a fierce small Irish boy to hand; but, thank goodness! there are still red Deepings left in England."

"What is a red Deeping?" said Mrs. Gibson.

"The red Deepings are an old East Anglian strain—red-haired and very fierce and cantankerous when roused. My little cousin Pollyooly here is a red Deeping."

"Oh, do you think she could cope with that horrid little boy?" said Mrs. Gibson eagerly.

"I'm sure of it," said the Honourable John Ruffin with decision. "Come here, Pollyooly."

Pollyooly came; and he felt her biceps carefully. Then he said:

"Didn't Mr. Vance tell me a story of a boy called Henry Wiggins whom you found disrespectful and taught manners?"

Pollyooly flushed faintly; but she said bravely, in an explanatory tone:

"I had to. He was always bothering."

"I should think that Henry Wiggins was a far more active and difficult boy in a fight than this fat little prince," said the Honourable John Ruffin.

"Oh, Henry Wiggins is tough but really he is quite easy. You've only got to get hold of his hair," said Pollyooly quickly. "But of course the prince has very short hair, only he isn't tough at all," she added in the grave tones of one weighing the chances of battle.

"He certainly is cropped. The Prussians have no aesthetic sense," said the Honourable John Ruffin in a disparaging tone. "But I should think that you could get over the difficulty of the hair."

"Oh, yes: I'm nearly sure I could," said Pollyooly; and her deep blue eyes began to shine. "May I smack him if he interferes with us?"

"Not on any account unless I am at hand," said the Honourable John Ruffin quickly. "I have a deep, patriotic distrust of the chivalry of Prussian barons. I do not think that this one could be trusted to see fair play. You might have a baron on your hands as well as a prince; and it might be too much for a red Deeping of your size. A prince at a time should be your motto."

"It would be very amusing," said Mrs. Gibson; and her eyes danced.

"You shall see it," said the Honourable John Ruffin amiably. "Unbiased spectators of a dramatic scene are always desirable; and it won't be difficult to arrange your presence, for the business will need a little stage-managing. You watch the prince, Pollyooly, and see how far he goes down the beach, so that we can arrange the exact place for his instruction."

The next day Pollyooly followed the prince to the end of his royal progress twice; and she had little doubt that she would be able to draw him into the battle for which she yearned, for he never saw her without scowling darkly upon her.

On the second day the Honourable John Ruffin returned from his golf in time to lunch with the two children; and he informed Pollyooly that he proposed to spend the afternoon on the sand with them. They found Mrs. Gibson with her children; and she accompanied them to the spot at which the

Edgar Jepson

prince usually turned in his course. Twenty yards beyond it the Honourable John Ruffin bade Pollyooly build a castle; and then he and Mrs. Gibson left her and the Lump to build it, and retiring to the sea-wall forty yards away, they sat down and fell into polite conversation. As they left her, the Honourable John Ruffin's last words to Pollyooly were:

"I don't forbid you to scratch him. Scratching is harmonious with the female nature."

The statement afforded Mrs. Gibson grounds for the beginning of their polite conversation.

Pollyooly and the Lump worked steadily away at the building of the castle. Pollyooly did the digging; now and again the Lump would pat a wall placidly. They had been at work for rather more than half an hour; and the castle was already beginning to wear the rotund air so dear to the eye of the builder when the progressive prince came in sight.

Pollyooly's joyful heart began to beat quickly. He was slouching along to his doom nearly fifty yards in front of the fragrant baron; and since there were children to annoy all the way, he came but slowly. It gave Pollyooly time to lead the Lump half-way to Mrs. Gibson, and send him toddling the rest. She was back at her castle, and at work again when the prince caught sight of her.

He stopped short, his unhasty mind slowly taking in the situation. That she should be working in loneliness, thirty yards beyond the line of nurses and children along the beach, seemed too good to be true. Presently his unhurrying mind grasped the fact that it was true; his heart blazed in his bosom; he threw back his head and, had his nose been larger, he would have sniffed the breeze like a warhorse. He advanced upon her in a quick, shambling slouch.

Pollyooly saw his eager advance; but she affected not to see it. She was eager for the fray, but fearful lest a display of that eagerness should dash the royal courage; moreover she wished the prince to be flagrantly the aggressor. She worked at the farther wall of the castle with her back to him. A fray was the last thing the prince looked for. There had been but one fray in his sheltered life: with a brother prince carelessly admitted to his society. A fray with a child not of the blood royal was beyond dreaming. He sprang on to the castle wall and began to stamp and kick a breach in it with furious, but clumsy, energy.

Then Pollyooly turned and sprang. The prince was hardly aware of her spring; he was only aware of a stinging smack, and then the shock of her impetus toppled him over on to his back on the sand. Pollyooly came down too, but not on the sand; she came down on the prince, and far more heavily than her fragile air warranted. Before he could collect any scattered wits he may have chanced to have, she was kneeling astride him, with a painful, grinding knee on either of his arms, and slapping his face.

The Honourable John Ruffin walked briskly down from the sea-wall with a smile of profound pleasure on his face. The perfumed baron had not yet perceived his charge's plight.

Pollyooly did not smack very hard at first, for she was resisting the wriggling of the prince; but once she had dug her toes firmly into the sand, she gave her mind to delivering each smack with the full swing of her arm; and the prince began to bellow. Then the baron saw the terrible, treasonable indignity the hope of the house of Lippe-Schweidnitz was enduring. He broke into a curious toddling run, uttering odd, short shrieks of the last horror as he came.

The Honourable John Ruffin placed himself athwart the

Edgar Jepson

course of the toddling deliverer and said quietly:

"Don't hurry, Pollyooly, but smack him hard."

A smile of understanding wreathed Pollyooly's flushed but angel face; and she did smack him hard. The Honourable John Ruffin's back was turned to the headlong baron; but his head was bent a little sideways; and as the already breathless rescuer made his final spurting rush he moved sharply to the left.

It was unfortunate (but since he had not eyes in the back of his head, it could not be helped) that the left shoulder of the Honourable John Ruffin, jerking upward hard, should have impinged upon the onrushing right shoulder of the deliverer. The baron left the firm earth, twirled in the air in a fashion which would have won him the plaudits of the most exacting music-hall audience, came down on his back on the sand with a violence which shook the little breath left out of his body and lay gasping in a darkened world.

It was a full minute and a half before the bellowing of his sufficiently besmacked charge came again, dimly, to his comprehending ears. Then he grew aware, also dimly, that the Honourable John Ruffin was standing over him and asking loudly, with every appearance of just indignation, what he meant by not looking where he was going. The baron was strongly of the opinion that the interposed shoulder had been no accident; but he was much too busy with his breathing to say so. Then when his breath came more easily and he had the power to say so, he had no longer the inclination, for the knowledge of the terrible position in which he stood, or rather lay, had flashed on him: he, a German officer, had been knocked down by a civilian and was forever disgraced.

Pollyooly continued to smack the bellowing prince; the Honourable John Ruffin continued to ask the baron what the devil he meant by it; and the poor wits of the panting nobleman continued to work on his dreadful problem. Then a flash of inspiration showed him the saving solution: he could accept his noisy questioner's view that his fall had been an accident. He sat up and began to apologise faintly and sulkily for having been knocked down.

The hands of Pollyooly were sore from smacking Prince Adalbert, but not so sore as his royal cheeks; and still she smacked on. She interjected between the smacks requests for an assurance that he would cease to annoy the children on the beach. His fine Prussian determination not to be robbed of his simple pleasures prevented him from giving it. He preferred to bellow. But there are limits even to royal endurance; and as the baron rose shakily to his feet, the prince howled the assurance she demanded.

"And mind you do, or I'll smack you again," said Pollyooly coldly.

She rose to her feet, flushed and triumphant, and rubbed gently together her stinging hands. The prince lay where he was, blubbering.

Ten yards away Mrs. Gibson stood holding the hand of the Lump, who gazed at the scene in placid wonder; and she was laughing gently. Ten yards away, on her right, stood a dozen children, surveying their blubbering pest with joyful, vengeful eyes. Behind them distractedly hovered three shocked nurses, quivering with horror at the upheaval of the social edifice; and horror-stricken mothers were slowly approaching the dreadful spot.

The baron slowly took in the humiliating significance of the scene; he saw that the glory of a royal house had been levelled to the dust, or rather to the sand. He caught his blubbering charge by the arm, jerked him to his feet, and led him away by one large ear.

The Honourable John Ruffin looked after them and laughed quietly but joyfully. Then he said:

"I congratulate you, Pollyooly—an excellent piece of work very neatly done. The haughty foreigner will trouble you no more."

Mrs. Gibson came forward and added her congratulations to his. The children gazed at Pollyooly with deep respect. Only the nurses and the mothers held aloof; an earthquake shock would hardly have astonished and confused them more than had this smacking of royalty. Had any one but the little cousin of the Honourable John Ruffin smacked, they would have been unable to refrain from an outburst of open disapproval.

To judge from the royal progress next morning, Pollyooly had indeed done her work. The Baron von Habelschwert still perfumed the air as he walked; but it was no longer obviously the air of a conquered country. His moustache was less fierce, his stride less proprietary. Indeed he might easily have been mistaken, by those to whom his name and dignities were unknown, for the pear-shaped but inoffensive keeper of a delicatessen shop. Prince Adalbert of Lippe-Schweidnitz was also changed. He no longer roamed afield; he kept within six feet of his protective equerry. He slouched less; and he had ceased to scowl arrogantly on the children who no longer fled at his approach. He regarded little English girls with a respectful, not to say timid, eye, and edged closer to the baron as he passed one. To his mind the little English girl was stored with the potentialities of a powder-magazine.

CHAPTER XIII

THE RAPPROCHEMENT

The noble-hearted humanitarian is ever of the opinion that violence, physical violence, is degrading alike to those who employ it, and to those on whom it is employed. In the main, doubtless, he may be right; but there must be natures, exceptional natures, on which it does not exercise this disastrous effect; and it is curious that there should be two human beings in so small a place as Pyechurch at the same time of this very nature.

There can be no doubt that Pollyooly had smacked Prince Adalbert of Lippe-Schweidnitz with far greater violence than ever she had smacked the abhorred Henry Wiggins for yelling "Ginger!" at her. There can be no doubt that the prince had been so smacked. Yet Pollyooly's face remained the face of an angel child; her devotion to the Lump and her politeness to those with whom she came into contact showed no signs of weakening; and no one could honestly assert that Prince Adalbert looked a bit more like a pig than he had always done. If anything he had lost something of his likeness to that nutritious animal.

At any rate there was no sign of degradation in his behaviour. He now walked about Pyechurch beach as peacefully as you could wish: he destroyed no castles; he kicked no children.

Even that fierce, stout, moustachioed and military Prussian, the Baron von Habelschwert, seemed to have derived benefit from his violent impingement on the left shoulder of the Honourable John Ruffin. Though his more mature nature should have been fixed, there can be no doubt that he wore a softer air, and no longer trod the English sand with the air of a disdainful but perfumed conqueror.

He was by no means an observant man; but stupid as he was, he could not fail to perceive the change in his pupil, for it was forced on his attention by the fact that the prince did not kick his shins for seventy-two hours. The baron was at first surprised, then dismayed: he feared that the fine Hohenzollern spirit of his young charge might have suffered a lasting, weakening shock from his encounter with that angel child; and when the prince for three successive mornings and afternoons did not assault a single little girl, however much smaller than himself those who came within his reach chanced to be, the fear deepened.

Oddly enough the subdued prince did not seem to regard Pollyooly with the bitterness which might have been expected. He did not even shun the sight of her. Indeed, as he made his royal progress along the beach, he would pause and regard her with puzzled but manifestly quite respectful interest, as she played actively not far from her little brother, the Lump, with her young friends.

The baron regarded the Honourable John Ruffin in a very different manner; he could not set eyes on him without scowling horribly. It was the desire of his heart to have the blood of Pollyooly's protector; and though the conduct of Pollyooly had oddly but considerably weakened his confident expectation of the immediate subjugation of the English people by his imperial master he longed with a greater fervour than had ever before burned in him for THE DAY.

The conversations, strictly confined to the British tongue, between the baron and his pupil, were always of the briefest and often truculent. The prince was a silent child, by reason of the fact that he had nothing to say. But one morning as they came down to the beach he startled the baron by saying:

"I want to blay."

"Yes, 'ighness, whad shall we blay ad?" said the Baron von Habelschwert uncomfortably, after a little hesitation.

"I don't want to blay wiz you," said the prince in a tone which showed, beyond any possibility of misconception, that on that matter his mind was made up.

"Bud zere's no one else for you do blay wiz," said the baron in English.

"I want to blay wiz childrens," said the pupil.

The baron drew his heels together and became, though still pear-like, splendidly rigid. His eyes flashed with haughty, but a trifle vicarious pride, as he said:

"Zere are no children for your 'ighness do blay wiz 'ere. Zese are nod 'igh and well-born ones."

"I do nod care," said the prince in the tone of one who knew his own mind quite well.

"Id is imbossible," said the baron in a tone of finality.

The rhinocerine eyes of his little charge flashed in sudden wrath; and he uttered a curious, pig-like snort as he sprang at the baron, and got in one severe kick on his left shin before that thoughtless Prussian, who should have known so well what to expect, could abate his rigidity and bend forward and hold him off at the length of his arms. He well knew that, in that constrained attitude to his bellowing pupil, he was presenting no dignified spectacle. None the less he was aware that he was affording considerable entertainment to the visitors taking the air on the sea-wall above him; and his joy in his young charge was not increased by the fact that among those visitors the Honourable John Ruffin smiled on the scene with amiable interest.

Having ascertained beyond all doubting that his well-shod toes could not reach the shins of his preceptor, the young prince ceased his futile effort, and with a most ungracious air moved along the beach. The limping baron followed him gloomily, with itching fingers. He felt that, in spite of the fact that his imperial master would shortly sweep her land with fire and sword from sea to sea, the lot of the happy English child Pollyooly was to be envied, since she could, and did, smack princes, with a mind untroubled by the sense of their sacrosanctity. Moreover he felt a sad prescience that his young charge, careless of the magnificent blood that flowed in his veins, *would* play with these children, who were neither high nor well-born. But he was quite unprepared for the actual group of children his young charge chose for playmates. He passed no less than four animated and excited groups before he arrived at that adorned and ruled by Pollyooly.

It chanced that it had decided to play rounders, and was gathered into an excited knot in which everybody was discussing, all at the same time, the process of picking sides.

The prince, shouldering aside, with proud Hohenzollern manliness, two or three little girls, thrust into the centre of the group and said:

"I want do blay."

The debating voices hushed; the other children stared at him with startled eyes, then drew aside leaving him face to face with Pollyooly.

"We don't want him to play with *us*!" cried Kathleen, who occupied the position of chief friend to Pollyooly.

"No, we don't!" cried the two other little girls.

The prince paid no heed to them; he looked at Pollyooly and said:

"I want do blay."

Pollyooly considered him thoughtfully, weighing the question of his admission to their circle with the care it demanded. He was not very pleasant to look at since he was so podgy, snub-nosed, pasty-faced, and small-eyed; but Pollyooly, mindful of their late encounter, and inspired by the magnanimity of the victor, did not at once reject the appeal.

"Will you promise to behave properly, if we let you play with us?" she said coldly.

The Baron von Habelschwert, standing over the group and nervously twirling his fierce moustache, shuddered and groaned. It was bad enough that his young, but pig-headed Hohenzollern should play at all with children who were neither high, nor well-born; but that he should only be admitted to play with them on terms passed the limit of human decency. He had read often in the sterner, but agrarian, papers of his Fatherland, that, owing to the increase of the Socialist vote, the world was coming to an end. He felt its once so solid mass trembling beneath his feet.

But the hope of the house of Lippe-Schweidnitz, insensible to the tremor, said eagerly:

"Yes."

"All right: then we'll try letting you play with us and see," said Pollyooly.

There came a faint murmur of protest from her friends, or rather from her followers; and she added with comforting assurance:

"Oh, it's all right; you needn't worry about him; I'll see that he behaves, myself."

With that assurance they were content—they had to be; the prince was admitted to the circle; and Pollyooly picked him on her side.

It had the first innings; and the baron expected the prince to be put in first. He was annoyed to observe that, as a mere matter of tactics, since she was by far the fastest of her side, that Pollyooly took that position herself. He was further annoyed when she put in her friend Kathleen next, an act of sheer favouritism unjustified by Kathleen's capacity; and after Kathleen she put in a little boy, and then another little girl. As they played their innings, she stood beside the prince and instructed him in the game. Once, since he appeared slow to grasp her meaning, she caught him by the shoulder and shook him to make it clearer. The Baron von

Habelschwert ground his teeth. When at last the prince did go in, the baron's heart swelled with proud expectation: his gallant little charge would display to those English children (they were neither high, nor well-born) the natural superiority of his royal blood and race.

The prince, however, did not fulfil this loyal expectation. He hit the ball, indeed, and in obedience to Pollyooly's shriek of instruction, started to run. But he started to run the wrong way round. His side shrieked as one child, as Pollyooly sprang upon him, swung him round, and shoved him along in the right direction. She succeeded in arresting his mad course at the first base by one of the shrillest shrieks of "Stop!" that ever burst from human lung. The next time the ball was hit she set him going again by a companion shriek; and with others of a like piercing quality (they seemed to flow from her lungs in an inexhaustible abundance) she guided him safely round the bases and home. From the blundering, stumbling way he ran, her shrieks seemed to be the only things in the world of which he was really conscious.

The baron watched the confused performance of his little charge with a strong feeling that something very serious indeed was the matter with the order of nature. When Pollyooly's side went out to field, he was no more satisfied by the prince's performance. Whenever the ball came to him, in spite of the fact that an encouraging, instructive shriek from Pollyooly reached him first, he either missed it, or fumbled it; and he always shied it in short. The baron's feeling that there was something very wrong with the cosmos grew stronger. He became depressed and yet more depressed by the fact that the prince was playing to an audience; for all the respectful and admiring nurses edged down the beach to behold him play; and those of them whose little charges were playing in the same game with him, assumed insufferable airs.

After a while the children tired of rounders and betook themselves to building a sand-castle. Since he had been admitted to their circle on her instance, Pollyooly seemed to feel herself responsible for the prince. She seemed also to feel it more important that he should learn to dig properly than that she should dig herself. For, giving him her spade, she stood over him and urged him to ply it with the exacting persistence of a biblical Egyptian superintending the making of bricks. The baron walked moodily up and down outside the castle wall, considering bitterly the while the defects in the cosmos.

The morning sped; and the prince perspired. At last the punctual baron observed that it was time to return home to lunch. In fact his vigilant stomach apprised him of the fact before his watch.

He came close to the castle wall and said:

"It's time for your Highness to coom 'ome."

His highness took no notice of him.

In a louder tone the baron said:

"Coom along, your Highness. Id's dime we go 'ome."

His highness shot a savage glance at him out of the corner of his eye, hunched his shoulders, and went on digging.

"Don't you hear the baron calling you, Prince?" said Pollyooly in a tone of some displeasure.

His highness seemed likely to withdraw his head right out of sight between his shoulders, and went on digging. He was still perspiring.

"Now you go along at once—like a good boy!" said Pollyooly sharply.

His highness raised his disappearing head and saw the cold resolve in her deep-blue eyes. He gave himself a little shake, stuck his spade into the sand, stretched his neck and went: but not like a good boy. He stumbled down the castle wall with his teeth set very tight, and immediately on reaching level ground kicked the shins of his unprepared preceptor. The baron, as was his wont, bent like a bow and held his little charge out at the length of his arms beyond the range of his shins, till his wrath should have abated.

Pollyooly's face filled with horror; she came springing lightly down the castle wall; cried: "Don't do that, you naughty little boy!" and caught the prince a resounding slap on the cheek.

The pent-up feelings of the prince escaped in a loud yell. He loosed his preceptor and pressed a hand to his stinging cheek.

It was too much for the baron. He tore his hat from his head, flung it to earth, ground it into the earth with his heel, and flung his arms to heaven in one frenzied movement:

"Ach Gott!" he cried to the unregarding sky. "Thad a liddle Eengleesh-she-devil-child should strike a Hohenzollern!"

Moved by his emotion, Pollyooly looked at him in anxious surprise:

"It's all right," she said in a soothing voice. "You don't know how to manage him. He'll go like a lamb."

Her surmise (it could have been no more than a surmise)

Edgar Jepson

proved accurate. The prince went blubbering, but he went like a lamb.

It might be supposed that his proud, Hohenzollern blood would have boiled for hours at the blow. Nothing of the kind.

After a hearty lunch he rose and said firmly:

"I'm going to blay wiz Bollyooly."

He went. The baron followed him gloomily. Now he knew the cosmic all to be a mere time-honored cheat.

In this order they came down on to the beach and approached a group of children in which Pollyooly reigned. The prince entered it with the air of an uninvited guest, very doubtful of his welcome, and said to Pollyooly in a tone half assertive, half beseeching:

"I've coom to blay."

Pollyooly looked at him with very stern eyes and said: "Well, you quite understand you've got to behave yourself."

The baron groaned.

Pollyooly turned to him and said with polite interest:

"Has he kicked you again?"

"Ach Himmel!" said the baron; and he thrust his hands into his pockets, clenched his fingers very tightly, and walked away with bowed head.

CHAPTER XIV

THE TRAINING OF ROYALTY

On that day began the real instruction of Prince Adalbert of Lippe-Schweidnitz in the art of life and the graces of social intercourse. Pollyooly continued it with unswerving firmness. Her method of treating a Hohenzollern was indeed entirely subversive of all current ideas on the matter of the deference due to the members of a family which has practically made the history of Europe since the beginning of this century. It seemed at times as if to her a Hohenzollern was a hardly animate object which you shoved here and there as you might an easy-chair which kept catching in the carpet, or at other times a mere beast of burden which you shoved, or shook, or cuffed gently into doing what you wanted with a moderate, but uncertain, degree of precision. Often however a piercing shriek was sufficient to produce the required action.

The prince was always in a perspiration, and often out of breath. But he seemed to thrive on the treatment: his appetite improved; his pastiness lessened; his skin grew clearer; and his flesh became less abundant and harder. He also became quicker in his movements, and showed many more glimmerings of intelligence, sometimes sustained for seconds at a time.

The baron's deferential soul could not endure the situation; and it never occurred to him to make the enquiries which would have informed him that Pollyooly, as a red Deeping, was of an older strain than the Hohenzollerns. He made many efforts to withdraw the prince from her society. He remonstrated both with her and with his little charge on the extraordinary impropriety of their being acquainted. But they seemed to find it entirely natural; and his efforts were vain. The prince, in truth, followed Pollyooly about; and what he followed her about like was a dog. He did not indeed spring to do her bidding, for he was not built to spring; but it was plain that if he could have sprung he would.

Perhaps the most remarkable fact about him was the improvement in his spirits: he was losing his air of gloomy savagery; often he smiled—at a dish which took his fancy, and on setting out for the sands to join Pollyooly. At times, when he had performed some small feat, clumsily indeed, but not with a quite incredible clumsiness, he would turn to her a triumphant, but appealing, eye which begged for a word, or a smile of approval. The humane Pollyooly rarely failed to give him that word or smile to brace him to fresh efforts. With other little girls he had come to be civil but uninterested; and little boys he ignored.

There are minds to whom it would have occurred that there were other seaside resorts equally healthy with Pyechurch to one of which the young prince might be removed to save him from the social degradation of playing with children who were neither high, nor well-born. The baron's was not one of these minds: he was a soldier of the emperor; he had been instructed that his young charge was to spend a month at Pyechurch; at Pyechurch he must spend it. But he wrote a long and earnest letter to his august master, the Grand Duke of Lippe-Schweidnitz, informing him, with full details, of his son's unfortunate social entanglement with a red-haired

English child, and of the impossibility, in the circumstances, of his putting an end to it. He got no answer, for the grand duke was splendidly busy maintaining the agrarian interests of his Fatherland. The baron therefore found himself compelled to accept the situation gloomily. Presently he was accepting it with resignation. He found that Pollyooly lightened his work. She relieved him of his little charge for the greater part of the day. He could now carry a deck-chair on to the sands, and stretched at full length in it, with a large, but not extravagantly fragrant, cigar in his mouth, could spend the sunny hours in the perusal of the works of the English novelists who appealed most strongly to his idealistic Teutonic sensibilities.

Sometimes however he was disturbed in this resigned acceptance of the situation. One afternoon he raised his head from the enthralled perusal of "Maiden Sweet" to find that the sands were empty of his charge. He struggled up from his chair, dropped the luscious masterpiece into it, and hurried in search of him. Pollyooly was a good sixty yards away; and he was breathless when he reached her. He clamoured wheezily for information as to the whereabouts of the prince. Pollyooly told him, indifferently enough, that he had gone to the village. The baron sought the village at his best, but curious, toddling rush. In the middle of it he met his young charge plodding along with an air of perfect content. In his hand he bore a paper bag.

"Vot 'af your 'ighness been doing?" cried his richly purple preceptor.

"Bollyooly zent me to buy bebbermints," said his charge stolidly, without stopping.

"Mein Gott!" cried the baron. "And now that she-devil-child uses you as a lackey!"

"She wanted zem," said his charge stolidly, pursuing his way without turning his head.

"Bud bebbermints you do not like!" cried the baron.

"Bollyooly wanted bebbermints," said the prince stolidly.

The baron said no more because there was no more to say.

He followed his charge to the beach and sought his chair; his charge sought Pollyooly. Gloomily the baron resumed his perusal of "Maiden Sweet." He had not read half a page when the thoughtful Pollyooly sent the prince to offer him a peppermint. The baron refused it with the proper cold scorn. The prince put it into his own mouth.

"Bud bebbermints you do not like!" said the baron again.

"Bollyooly says bebbermints is goot," said the prince stolidly; and he turned on his heel.

The baron searched the far-smiling sea with wild, questioning eyes. It offered neither explanation nor comfort.

It chanced a few days later that the Honourable John Ruffin put Pollyooly's skilful cooking to the further test of grilling mushrooms along with his bacon. They came from the marsh. Presently to Pollyooly's prudent mind it seemed foolish to pay for vegetables which might be gathered for nothing. She resolved to gather them herself; and one afternoon with that end in view she came down to the sands, leading the Lump, and carrying a basket, and suggested to Kathleen and others of her young friends that they should accompany her on her quest and share the spoil. But their nurses, fore-seeing extra work from the mud in the marsh, would not allow them to go.

The prince, who had been waiting patiently for the arrival of Pollyooly, while the baron slept in his deck-chair, listened to the discussion with uncomprehending ears. It did not occur to her to invite the be-tutored Hohenzollern to accompany her; but when she started, the prince, doubtful of the reception of a direct offer to escort her would receive, followed her at a distance of about thirty yards. Pollyooly was giving her attention to the Lump, and was not aware of her follower until she had crossed the bridge over the dyke, from the road into the marsh. There she turned and saw him; and at the first sight of him she was minded to send him back to his sleeping tutor. Then it occurred to her that the company of the prince would be better than no company at all; and she suffered him to come.

Though neither of them had any conversation, Pollyooly talked away to the prince and the Lump, and was quite content with the grunts of assent with which the prince punctuated her observations. But she was presently annoyed to find that he shone no more as an assistant mushroomer than as a conversationalist. It was not so much that he was ignorant of the difference between mushrooms and toads-tools, and equally unskilful in discovering either, as that he often trod on the fairest members of the group he was picking. Pollyooly therefore gave him the basket to carry and picked the mushrooms herself. Twice he dropped it and scattered them over the turf. She chid him but gently and carried it herself.

But destiny, which dogs the steps of princes, was leading him to a catastrophe. The basket was large and growing heavy; but the indefatigable Pollyooly pushed deeper into the marsh. They had crossed several dykes safely; then they came to a plank over a small dyke, nearly dried up. Pollyooly took every possible care to get the expedition across safely. She carried the Lump across and then the basket of mushrooms. Then she turned to watch the passage of the prince. The plank was not more than ten feet long; and it was destiny which chose the exact middle of it for the prince to fall off. He struck the dyke with a splash which drew a cry of delight from the Lump, and sank up to his knees in the thick mud. He burst into a terrified bellow; and Pollyooly hurried down the steep bank to help him out. But destiny had arranged that he should be just out of her reach; and he was too frightened to make the effort to struggle to her helping hand.

For a while Pollyooly, for all her power of resource, was at a loss; and the bellowing of the prince did nothing to clear her wits. Then she saw how she could reach him. She dug her feet into the bank, hugged the plank over the dyke with her left arm, and leaning forward, succeeded in getting a grip of his left wrist, and began to tug. Her grip seemed to inspirit him, for he began to struggle hard toward the bank. It was not an easy business in the thick mud, but thanks to the purchase afforded by the plank, Pollyooly could put most of her strength into the effort and slowly dragged him on to the firmer mud at the edge and then on to the bank.

Still blubbering a little, he followed Pollyooly up the bank; on the top of it she turned and surveyed him with horrified eyes. He was wrapped nearly up to his waist in a smooth, dripping garment of greenish mud; and patches of it adorned the rest of him. It would have been difficult to imagine anything more unlike a Hohenzollern in a white sailor suit; and his face was hardly attractive enough to justify you in comparing him to the dripping, weed-be-draped Lorelei of his native land.

"Well! You *are* an aggravating little boy! Whatever am I to do with you?" cried Pollyooly in a tone of despair.

The prince uttered an apologetic grunt.

"The only thing to do is to get you home as quick as I can," she said heavily.

She carried the Lump back across the dyke, then the basket of mushrooms. Then she led the prince across it. They took their slow way back to the village, the prince leaving behind him a trail which would have gladdened the heart of the last, or any other, of the Cherokees.

The Baron von Habelschwert, sleeping peacefully beside a sweet work of genius, called "Dove Wifie," which had fallen from his hand, missed the departure of his young charge in the wake of Pollyooly. He slept for an hour; and when he did awake, her friends had moved a long way down the beach. He struggled to his feet, and set out in search of the prince, assured that he was somewhere on the sands playing with his active, but socially impossible, protector. At first he sought him with careless eyes, then with keener; but it was some twenty minutes before he satisfied himself that neither his charge nor Pollyooly were on the sands. Then he set out, in some annoyance to search the village; and when he had drawn blank all the village shops at which sweets were sold, he began to grow anxious and alarmed. For all his military contempt for the English as a people soon to be subjugated, he had a deep distrust of them. It awoke suddenly in its most violent form; and he began to suspect that the perfidious politicians of England had stolen his Hohenzollern.

The suspicion presently became a conviction; and he acted on it with splendid, but unwonted, energy. In little more than ten minutes the village was ringing with the news that the prince was lost; and the baron was toddling furiously along at the head of a band composed of the village children, the village idiot, some idle fishermen, and a number of unoccupied visitors who had leapt at the chance of action. There was no lack of theories. Every other member of the group had one of his own. The baron himself made no secret of his belief that the prince was the victim of a political plot, till the Honourable John Ruffin, out of mere idle curiosity, stopped the procession to enquire its object and on learning it proclaimed his firm conviction that the prince was neither lost, stolen, nor strayed.

By this time the news had spread to the sands; and a nurse came hurrying up with the information that the prince had gone into the marsh, mushrooming with Pollyooly.

"Ach Gott! Then that little she-devil-child haf 'im drowned in a dyke!" said the baron cheerfully.

The suggestion increased greatly the interest of his followers; and they accompanied him into the marsh eagerly. On that expanse figures are seen at a great distance; but the searchers had gone a long way into it before they caught sight of the children. At some distance the figures of Pollyooly and the Lump, and even the basket of mushrooms were plainly recognised. But what was that strange object which moved beside them? The baron and his band quickened their steps, Pollyooly still walked at the leisurely gait which suited the Lump.

It was not till he was within ten yards of them that the procession and the baron recognised his young charge. The procession began to laugh heartily.

The baron flung his arms to heaven and cried, or, to be exact, howled:

"Vhat is it you haf done ad 'im?"

"I didn't do anything!" cried Pollyooly with indignant heat. "He did it *himself*! He *would* fall into the dyke! He's the most aggravating little boy I ever knew!"

"You trow 'im into ze dyke! You id on purpose did!" cried the furious baron.

"Bollyooly didn't," said his little charge stolidly.

"Do try and have a little sense, Baron von Habelschwert," said the Honourable John Ruffin, smiling upon the hope of the house of Lippe-Schweidnitz. "Pollyooly wouldn't throw any one into dykes."

"Bud look at 'im!" cried the baron. "'e will the enteric fever haf!"

"Oh, no. He didn't get any water into his mouth," said Pollyooly quickly. "I made him open it and looked, because Mr. Ruffin told me the marsh water gave people fever. It's only mud on his clothes."

"Moodd! Onlie moodd!" howled the baron. "His cloze, zey are spoiled! Ze cloze of the bezd dailor of Schweidnitz!"

That was a misfortune which appealed deeply to Pollyooly. She looked at the spoiled suit of the prince very sadly, and said generously:

"Well, I'll give him half of the mushrooms—though really he didn't gather them; and I had to carry the basket."

"Mooshrooms!" howled the baron. "Vhat is mooshrooms wiz cloze? Zeze English, zey are all mad!"

In his emotion the baron had not kept his usual wary watch

on his young charge, and so failed to observe the light of battle gather and gleam in his eyes. But as he finished the prince sprang at him, cried angrily: "Bollyooly isn't!" and kicked him on the shin.

The kick was stiff and lacked its usual snap; but it was sufficiently vigorous to dislodge a good deal of the mud from the once white trouser-leg and bespatter the legs of the baron, who uttered a short howl and bent like a bow, holding off his little charge, and gazing wildly round the marsh. This time Pollyooly did not come to his aid; she gazed at him with a cold eye.

"It serves you right—talking like that about people when they try to make up," she said coldly.

The prince, encouraged by this quite unexpected approval, made another fine effort to plant a second kick of remonstrance on the shin of his preceptor. His foot missed it; but plenty of mud hit it.

"That's enough, Adalbert. Stop it!" said the magnanimous Pollyooly sharply.

Adalbert stopped it.

The baron ground his teeth at this new familiarity; but was glad to be loosed by his admonished charge; and the procession took its triumphant way back to the village.

The prince's valet was a long while cleaning him; but directly after his tea he was out on the sands again, seeking Pollyooly.

CHAPTER XV

THE ATTITUDE OF THE GRAND DUKE

The baron's bitterness was deepened by this accident to his charge; and he continued stubbornly to lay the blame of it on Pollyooly: if she had not actually flung him into the dyke, she had led him into the marsh, where the dyke was. Then two mornings later there came a telegram to inform him that the Grand Duke of Lippe-Schweidnitz, on his way to answer the letter of appeal in person, was already in London, and would reach Pyechurch early in the afternoon. The baron was a glad man. All the morning, reclined in his deck-chair, with eyes full of a gloating triumph, he watched Pollyooly direct the play of the prince; and as he watched he hummed an aria, the same aria, of Mozart. He foresaw a speedy end to this distressing social entanglement and her evil domination.

At lunch he informed his royal charge of the coming of his august sire, and told him that he must stay at home to welcome him.

"I go do blay wiz Bollyooly," said his young charge stolidly.

"You vill nod go," said the baron firmly.

His young charge said no more; he only looked at his beaming

Edgar Jepson

preceptor with eyes cold with the steeliest contempt. The baron failed to grasp the purport of the look.

After lunch he had the prince carefully cleaned, and then set him in an easy chair under his eye, to await the coming of his august sire, who would arrive about a quarter to three. Then he walked up and down the room working out the most effective presentation of his indictment of Pollyooly and the social entanglement. At intervals he gesticulated and muttered a phrase. He was making excellent progress with it and at five and twenty minutes to three he was at the end of it. The prince sat stolidly in the easy chair by the long windows. At twenty-four minutes to three the baron flung out the last damning phrase (with the appropriate splendid gesture) at his image in the looking-glass over the mantelpiece. Then he turned to beam triumphantly on his little charge. The easy chair was empty; the prince had gone.

With language far less sonorous, but more staccato, the baron bounced to the window, just in time to see his little charge disappear swiftly over the edge of the sea-wall fifty yards away. Unfortunately the baron wore his hair too short to be able to tear handfuls of it from his head, or he would have bereft himself of a handful or two. But everything that language could do to ease him, language did. He must be at home to receive his august master: etiquette demanded it imperatively. He had no time to recover his young charge, whose presence etiquette demanded no less imperatively. Dashed from his height of splendid triumph, and exhausted by the fluency with which he had dealt with the appalling situation, he sank heavily into the easy chair, an embittered man.

He was quickly roused from his gloom by the stopping of a barouche before the house. In it sat his august master, a splendid round figure of a man, clad in the lightest-coloured tweeds Schweidnitz could boast, and surmounted by the whitest of white bowlers. His large, broad, square face ended in three well-moulded chins. In the middle of the fine expanse of face (his was not a high forehead) was a bristling imperial moustache, far fiercer than the baron's; above it rose a big, thick nose. His eyes were a bright blue; and they twinkled in an engaging fashion somewhat disappointing in a royal personage. Beside him sat a slim, contrasting equerry.

The baron rushed forth, and after the manner of his caste, was abject in his apologies for the absence of Prince Adalbert. . . . He had taken every precaution. . . . All had been in vain. . . . The infatuated unfortunate would steal away to the little she-devil-child.

"Ach, zo?" said the grand duke, who made a point of speaking English in England; and he descended with earth-shaking majesty from the creaking barouche.

"Ve vill go to zem," he said after testing the soil of Pyechurch with a cautious foot to make sure that it was equal to his weight.

On the way to the sea-wall the baron poured forth his damning indictment, disjointedly and without the fierceness of phrase and splendour of gesture he had practised; and three times the grand duke said, somewhat phlegmatically, the baron thought:

"Ach zo?"

They came out on to the wall just above the band of Pollyooly's subjects, hot and excited in a game of rounders.

The quick eye of the grand duke at once espied Prince Adalbert running to field a ball.

"Ach, he is zlimmer!" he said in a tone of satisfaction.

"Zlimmer? He is zlimmer, your Highness. Id iz zat leedle she-devil-child. She nevare—nod nevare—leds 'im be steel. All ze day she makes 'im roosh and roosh. He haf nevare no breath in hees loongs—nod nevare!"

"Ach, zo?" said the grand duke calmly. "He is rooning mooch faster zan he vas could."

"Id's zat leedle she-devil-child! She make 'im roon and roon all ze day!" cried the baron.

"Ach, zo?" said the grand duke. "Alzo he is peenk—guite peenk."

The satisfaction in his tone had increased. He could hardly be called a fond parent, in the matter of Adalbert; he might more truly be said to bear with him. Indeed he had never been able to explain the boy to his satisfaction. There was perhaps a slight physical resemblance between Adalbert and his parents; but whereas he knew himself to be one of the astutest princes in the German Empire and his wife to be an uncommonly clear-witted woman, no father's partiality hid from him the fact that Adalbert was obtuse. He was inclined to accept sadly the theory of Professor Muller, professor of anatomy and physiology at the University of Lippe-Schweidnitz, and court physician, that Adalbert cast back to his great-grandfather Franz, who had been known to his irreverent subjects as "The Dolt."

He gazed at the perspiring and excited band for a minute in silence. Then he said:

"Wheech is ze leedle she-devil-child?"

"Zat von—zat von in ze meedle—wiz ze red 'air," said the baron.

He pointed to Pollyooly in the middle of the ring where she was acting as pitcher, her face flushed, her eyes shining, her red hair a flying cloud.

An immense slow smile spread over the expanse of royal face; and the grand duke cried: "Mein Gott! Bud id is nod a child at all—zat! Id is an anchel—a leedle anchel—Italian renascence! Is id nod, Erkelenz?" And he turned to his slim equerry.

"Yes, Highness: authentic," said the equerry.

The Baron von Habelschwert gasped; he could not believe his ears.

The little girl, batting, whacked the ball over the prince's head.

"Run, Adalbert! Run!" shrieked Pollyooly.

"Roon, Adalbert! Der Teufel! Roon!" bellowed the grand duke.

It is hard to say whether the shriek of Pollyooly or the terrific bellow of his august sire was the sharper spur to the prince's legs; but he saved the rounder.

"Sblendid! 'e did not roon like an ox," said the grand duke almost proudly. "Vhat did you write vas ze name of zat leedle anchel?"

"Bollyooly, your Highness," gasped the baron in a feverish doubt whether he was standing on his head or his heels, for the grand duke had heard her call the hope of the house of Lippe-Schweidnitz "Adalbert" with his own ears!

"Bollyooly? A beautiful name!" cried the grand duke with enthusiasm.

Then came the great event of Prince Adalbert's life. The little boy who was batting hit the ball right into his hands. He grabbed at it; and by a miracle it stuck in his fingers.

His side leapt and shrieked as one child; and the grand duke leapt and bellowed. The shock of his descent on the sea-wall made it quiver for many feet round him.

He turned upon his slim equerry, seized his arm, and shook him as the wind shakes a blade of corn.

"Did you see zat? Id is ze creeket! 'e caught 'im out," he bellowed in stentorian tones which rang out far across the marsh. "Bollyooly has made 'im zlim! She has made 'im roon! She has made 'im peenk! She has taught 'im ze creeket! She shall rewarded be! I will gonfer on 'er ze Order of Chastity of Lippe-Schweidnitz of ze zecond class!"

He loosed his slim equerry, and hammered his enormous right palm with his huge left fist.

The slim equerry shook his head (this time without any assistance from his august master) and said:

"She is too young, your Highness. Ze order can only be gonferred on ladies of twenty-von or elder."

"Zen I will gonfer it on 'er when she is twenty-von! Bud I will reward 'er alzo now! Vetch 'er!" cried the grand duke.

The slim equerry went down the sea-wall across the sands to Pollyooly. The game stopped while he conferred with her. Pollyooly looked from him to the fine, round figure on the sea-wall; then she patted her hair, smoothed her frock, called to her young companions that she would be back in a minute or two, and went with the slim equerry. She was not timid, or even shy. Her estimate of the royal family of Lippe-Schweidnitz had been formed from her knowledge of Prince Adalbert; and it was not a high one. That royal family left her unimpressed and certainly unrevering. She was hardly curious about the grand duke.

On the way to him the slim equerry asked her her name, and told her to be sure to address the grand duke as "your Highness."

On the sea-wall he took her hand, grew rigid, saluted, and said:

"I present the Fraeulein Bollyooly von Bride to your Highness."

Like the well-mannered child she was, Pollyooly dropped a curtsey.

The grand duke seized her hand, and shook it warmly, and cried:

"Mein Gott! if you were zeven—five years elder, I would keess you! Bud id is far to sdoop. You haf done great good to my zon, ze Prince Adalbert. You haf made him peenk—guite peenk; and you haf taught him ze creeket. Id iz sblendid; and you moost rewarded be. Gif me my burse, Erkelenz."

The slim equerry took a purse from his pocket and handed it

to the grand duke. The grand duke opened it, turned it upside down, poured on to his palm eleven golden sovereigns, and pressed them with somewhat clumsy fingers into Pollyooly's hands.

The amazed Pollyooly flushed; and her eyes shone like bright stars; the family of Lippe-Schweidnitz rose a thousand feet in her estimation.

"Oh! Thank you, your Highness!" she gasped.

"Zere is no zanks—nod none! You haf made Adalbert peenk. You are von sblendid anchel child. And id iz me to zank you," said the grand duke; and very gently, for the size of his fingers, he patted her head. Then he drew himself up and, with a splendid wave of his gigantic hand, added:

"Und now go and blay wiz Adalbert—blay wiz him always!"

CHAPTER XVI

POLLYOOLY ENTERTAINS ROYALTY

Pollyooly came away from the presence of the grand duke in something of a daze. She came down the steps in the sea-wall quite unconscious of the fact that she was not moving over level ground. The eleven golden sovereigns in her hand felt too good to be true; and at the bottom of the steps she stopped and counted them with eyes which could hardly believe what they saw: eleven golden sovereigns.

She gave them into the care of Mrs. Gibson while, in obedience to the behest of the grand duke, she continued to play rounders.

The game had fallen into a state of suspended animation during her absence from it. Her return enlivened it. Presently she was again absorbed in it, playing it with the concentration with which she did most things, the concentration which is so large a part of genius, which made her one of the finest grillers of bacon in England. She forgot the grand duke; she forgot the eleven golden sovereigns; she thought only of the game; and she drove her team and the perspiring prince with merciless vigor.

The grand duke watched it closely, now and then applauding

Edgar Jepson

in an excited, ringing voice. Prince Adalbert had performed his one great exploit and was now declined upon a lower level. He played his best, obeying with his natural clumsiness the shrieked commands of Pollyooly; but he did not again arise to a really meritorious feat. Nevertheless, the grand duke was content with him.

He did not indeed watch him very closely; he had chiefly eyes for Pollyooly.

Once he said with enthusiasm:

"She is ze gompanion Adalbert 'af need of."

And again he said with enthusiasm:

"'ow it would be goot if she goom to Schweidnitz and blay wiz 'im all ze days, Erkelenz!"

The slim equerry shook his head and said in a tone of conviction:

"She would nod coom, Highness."

Being of a younger generation, he spoke better English than his royal master.

The grand duke shook his head sadly, and said;

"No: she would nod goom. Would she nod goom for mooch money, you zink?"

"I do nod zink she could be persuaded to coom," said his equerry.

"No: she would nod goom," said the grand duke. The baron

had an inspiration; he said in a stern voice:

"Ze day, 'ighness; ze day will goom soon. Zen you will gommand only; and Bollyooly will obey."

"Ach, yes: ze day," said the grand duke, watching the playing children. "It will goom soon doubtlez. Bud Bollyooly, will she obey? Zeze English blay zere creeket very 'ard."

"She would be made obey," said the baron firmly.

The grand duke changed the subject by raising his voice in a splendid, heartening roar at Pollyooly, who was running swiftly around the bases; and for nearly an hour he did his best to burst the welkin. Then he summoned the perspiring prince, shouted and waved good-bye to Pollyooly, and walked to his son's lodgings to take a little unnecessary nourishment before driving to the station.

Pollyooly went on playing till a quarter of five, when the game broke up to let the players go to their tea. She collected the Lump from the Gibson nurse and the eleven sovereigns from Mrs. Gibson, and started down the beach tea-wards. As she went down the beach several earnest enquirers stopped her to ask what the grand duke had said to her and what she had said to the grand duke. They wore the air of being very deeply impressed by the occurrence.

Pollyooly gratified their curiosity. Four of them said that they would have been so confused by being suddenly hurried into the presence of royalty that, not knowing whether they were standing on their heads or their heels, they would not have found a word to say.

Pollyooly said quite truly that she had not suffered from any such confusion. She did not add, as with no less truthfulness she might have done, that what had induced a slight access of confusion in her had been the sudden and unexpected possession of eleven golden sovereigns. But she had a feeling, somewhat obscure, that such a happening should not confuse a red Deeping; therefore she did not say anything about it.

She and the Lump were still at tea when the Honourable John Ruffin returned from his golf and joined them. She told him of the coming of the grand duke, of his thanks for the improvement in Prince Adalbert's health, and of the eleven splendid golden sovereigns.

"And very nice too. I congratulate you," said the Honourable John Ruffin cheerfully.

"Thank you," said Pollyooly.

"I always have heard that the grand duke is a very decent sort, as well as being astute; and this proves it," he said.

"But it does seem such a lot for the little I've done. I could have done a lot more, if I'd known," said Pollyooly in a tone of discomfort.

"Not a bit of it," said the Honourable John Ruffin in a confident tone. "As what you've done goes, eleven golden sovereigns isn't a penny too much for it. I haven't observed the treatment; but I have no doubt that you're making another boy of Prince Adalbert."

"Well, he does look better and he does get about quicker than he did," said Pollyooly slowly, weighing her words.

"Well, that's a good deal," said the Honourable John Ruffin in an encouraging tone.

"And he is a little brighter too, though he does only grunt; and of course he behaves better; he doesn't knock the other children about like he used to."

"Well, there you are," said the Honourable John Ruffin, in the tone of one completely satisfied.

"Oh, but he is slow!" Pollyooly protested. "It would take weeks and weeks to really do anything with him—weeks and weeks."

"But what can you expect?" said the Honourable John Ruffin amiably. "The red Deepings were notable people, ruling a county, and hacking and hewing the best people in four counties round, when the ancestors of the prince were swineherds in a Prussian forest. And those ancestors stayed in that forest for five hundred years after that. Prince Adalbert doesn't throw back more than a hundred and fifty years. If a red Deeping produced an Adalbert, he would throw back six hundred and fifty years; and it isn't done."

"Yes," said Pollyooly politely, though she did not follow at all his abstruse dissertation.

"So you see you needn't feel overpaid at all," he said.

"No," said Pollyooly in the tone of one perfectly satisfied.

"Besides, if you do, you can always put in a little more training."

"Oh, yes: that was what I was meaning to do," she said.

Now that Pollyooly had been approved, or rather enthusiastically welcomed, as the ideal companion of Prince Adalbert, the baron was all affability and winning smiles. He had indeed reason to be, for she made life much easier for him. Without a care he abandoned Prince Adalbert to her whenever she would have him, and sat reading or sleeping in his deck-chair on the sunny sands with a mind wholly at peace. With that approved guardian the prince must be safe.

Thus it came about that he became Pollyooly's perpetual companion, or, to be exact, her perpetual hanger-on. He could not be said to afford companionship to her, for, like the Lump, he preferred the grunt to articulate speech. He played in all the games in which she played—at least, if they were not too difficult for his understanding. If they were, he watched her play them with the dogged attention of an enthusiast.

As she came to know him better and better, it is to be feared that Pollyooly remembered his exalted station less and less. She quite forgot the prince in the boy. She sometimes deplored the fact to Mrs. Gibson that though Adalbert could now be trusted not to get into mischief by any act of will, he was so stupid that he needed a perpetual eye on him.

The Honourable John Ruffin sometimes enquired about his progress in morals, manners, and intelligence; Pollyooly's report on it was always dispirited. But he was surprised, on returning home from Littlestone to tea one evening, to find Pollyooly entertaining royalty in the parlour of the flustered Mrs. Wilson.

The prince had come back from a walk through the marsh with her, tired; and she had thought it better that he should have tea before walking the length of the village to his own lodging.

The Honourable John Ruffin did not let his surprise be seen; he greeted his royal guest civilly and sat down. Pollyooly questioned him closely and with genuine interest about his successes and reverses on the links. Then the Honourable John Ruffin observed that his royal guest was flushed; then he discovered that Pollyooly was entertaining him in a fashion at once negligent and drastic: she made no effort to include him in their talk, but she was watching him with the eye of a lynx and giving him a lesson in table manners with the coldest serenity.

"What is the matter with our royal guest exactly?" said the Honourable John Ruffin presently.

"He is so hard to teach," said Pollyooly plaintively. "You'd be surprised. I keep telling him not to eat like a pig; and for about four mouthfuls he doesn't. Then he forgets all about it; and I have to begin all over again."

The guilty flush deepened in the cheeks of the prince.

"You must give it time to sink in. He's not used to learning things; he has been so neglected," said the Honourable John Ruffin with a hospitable desire to make things easier for her royal guest.

Pollyooly shook her head doubtfully, and frowned sadly upon the prince.

"It would take weeks and weeks; and I don't really ever see him at meals," she said.

"Never mind: do what you can when you get the chance," said the Honourable John Ruffin in a heartening tone.

"That's what I must do," said Pollyooly; but there was no great hopefulness in her voice.

Edgar Jepson

Sadly she handed a plate of cake to Prince Adalbert. There was a sudden gleam in his small, but Hohenzollern, eye, and in one swift gesture he took, or rather, to be exact, grabbed a slice, and thrust a corner of it into his mouth.

As Pollyooly had said, for the first four bites all was well; but the next three were accompanied by a slushy noise such as arises in a pigstye at mealtime.

"There! There it is again!" she cried in tones of the bitterest protest. "Isn't it dreadful?"

The prince flushed a darker red and hushed the slushy accompaniment.

The Honourable John Ruffin looked sympathetically sad.

"I couldn't have believed that anybody could be so hard to teach a little thing like that to," said Pollyooly mournfully.

The prince grunted.

"Yes. I know you try to do your best—you needn't tell me that," said Pollyooly, who appeared to understand his syncopated Prussian. "But what is the good of a best like that?"

The prince finished the slice of cake with only two more slushy sounds. Pollyooly sighed once or twice; and tea came to an end.

They rose; and Pollyooly said with resolution:

"I see what I shall have to do. I shall have to look after his outdoor manners only."

CHAPTER XVII

THE DUKE HAS AN IDEA

Pollyooly did not again entertain royalty. She kept firmly to her resolve to superintend only the outdoor manners and behaviour of Prince Adalbert. She would not have her feelings again harrowed by his painfully exact rendering of the noises made by a sturdy, happy porker over its trough. But out of doors he continued, for the rest of her stay, to be her perpetual, noiseless, devoted, and generally perspiring squire.

That stay came to an end along with the Honourable John Ruffin's windfall. It had been a very pleasant stay; Pollyooly had enjoyed it more than any time of her life, more even than the days she had spent at Ricksborough Court when Lord Ronald Ricksborough had come there from Eton to spend his holidays. She was a little doubtful (for all that they were engaged to be married when she should have grown up and fitted herself to become the wife of an English peer by dancing for a while in musical comedy) whether the days at Pyechurch would be more pleasant if he were there, for he would naturally take the place of leader, and she was very happy in that position herself.

She wrote only one letter, a brief letter, to him from

Pyechurch, for she was really too busy to write more often (at the Temple she wrote at least once every ten days) and he wrote back to say that he wished he were with her instead of mugging away at his beastly work in his stuffy study. His letter brought home to Pollyooly the great advantage she had over richer children in having years ago passed the seven standards at the Muttle Deeping school, and so done with tedious school-books for good and all.

It was a sad day for her and the Lump when their stay at Pyechurch came to an end; but it was an even sadder day for Prince Adalbert. He was losing the one friend he had ever made, the only person in the world for whom he felt a warm admiration and a genuine respect—as warm an admiration indeed as his somewhat limited spirit was capable of feeling. It was not able to attain to the great heights of emotion; but to such a height of grief as it could rise to, it rose. As for his display of that grief, had he been a pretty boy the onlookers could not have failed to find it pathetic; as it was, for all that they were most of them keenly sensible of his royal condition, they were hard put to it not to find it grotesque.

Tears were not in keeping with his Hohenzollern face; and when he at last realised that Pollyooly was really going and for good, he bellowed like a very small, but broken-hearted bull.

A number of Pollyooly's friends and subjects had come to bid her good-bye; Prince Adalbert was no little hindrance to their farewells, for he had a tight grip on Pollyooly's skirt; and not only did his bellowing drown the sound of their voices but also he kept her chiefly busy trying to soothe him.

When at last she detached him from her skirt and bade him good-bye, and climbed into the wagonette, he tried to climb into it to go with her; and the Baron von Habelschwert had to lift him down and hold him firmly.

The wagonette drove off amid a loud chorus of farewells; and little given to the softer emotions as Pollyooly was, there were tears in her eyes as she looked back on the friends she was leaving. Her last sight of the prince was somewhat depressing: in a final access of despair he was kicking the baron's shins.

Pollyooly said, with far more indulgence than she had generally shown him:

"I don't suppose he'll break out like that very often."

"Still, after all your training, it is sad to see him massacring his faithful mentor," said the Honourable John Ruffin.

"Yes: it isn't nice of him," said Pollyooly without any great annoyance in her tone. "But really it's the baron's fault; he'd only have to smack him about twice."

"I expect he has conscientious scruples against smacking princes of the blood royal. Many people undoubtedly have," said the Honourable John Ruffin.

"Perhaps he has. But I think he'll miss me," said Pollyooly in a tone of sufficient satisfaction.

The baron would indeed miss her; and he was one of the saddest men in Pyechurch that day. With the departure of Pollyooly his hours of ease came to an end. No longer could he in his sunnily disposed deck-chair read the sweet books he loved in a perfect serenity. Once more he must follow his royal charge up and down the sands and keep an ever watchful eye on him.

The change from Pyechurch to the Temple was trying; but the unrepining Pollyooly soon grew used to it, though she missed for a while the wide spaces of the sea and marsh, and the inspiriting breezes from the sea.

The Honourable John Ruffin made some changes: she was to continue to call him John, or Cousin John; she was to do her work in gloves; and she was always to wear a large apron. The use of a large apron, though it might prevent her from working with her wonted speed, was to enable her to wear under it always a nice linen frock. Then, when any one knocked at the door of the chambers, she could slip off the apron, and let them in no longer in the guise of the Honourable John Ruffin's housekeeper, but as a member of his family.

He did not for a moment dream of relieving her altogether of her housework. In the first place he could not afford to do so; in the second place he thought it very good for her to be busy most of the day, and to feel that she was independent, earning her own living. He did not even bid her give up her post of housekeeper to Mr. Gedge-Tomkins. He was quite sure that a girl might have too little work to do, but he was very doubtful whether she could have too much.

Then he was talking one afternoon to Pollyooly, who had just made his tea and brought it to him; and she said:

"Who is Mr. Francis?"

"Mr. Francis who?" said the Honourable John Ruffin.

"I don't know," said Pollyooly, knitting her brow. "It was Mrs. Brown who talked about him. I took the Lump to see her the day after we came back from Pyechurch; and she said I was growing quite the lady."

"She would put it like that," said the Honourable John Ruffin sadly.

"And then she said that after all it wasn't to be wondered at, seeing who Mr. Francis was. But when I asked her what she meant, she wouldn't say any more."

The Honourable John Ruffin sat straighter up in his chair with a somewhat startled air. But he said in an indifferent enough tone:

"Ah, she grew mysterious, did she?"

"Ever so mysterious," said Pollyooly.

"It's a habit of her class, I believe," said the Honourable John Ruffin carelessly. "Probably she meant nothing at all."

Pollyooly went back to the Lump content; but the Honourable John Ruffin kept his brow puckered by a thoughtful frown for some time after she had gone. Then he shrugged his shoulders, and his face resumed its wonted serenity.

Three afternoons later there was a knocking at the door of the chambers; and Pollyooly opened it to find the Duke of Osterley standing on the threshold. She was surprised, because she had no reason to believe that the coldness which the Honourable John Ruffin had told her subsisted between himself and the duke had been dissipated; but, like the well-mannered child she was, she did not let her surprise be seen, but bowed politely as she had seen ladies at Pyechurch bow, for since she had been promoted to the position of the Honourable John Ruffin's cousin she had abandoned the curtsey as out of keeping with that more exalted station.

The duke gazed gloomily at her, for it was very present to his mind that their earlier meetings had, for him, been barren of joy; then he said gloomily:

"Ah, you *are* here. Is Mr. Ruffin back from the Law Courts yet?"

"No, your Grace; but he won't be long. He'll be back to tea in a minute or two: the clock's just struck four," she said; and she drew aside for him to enter.

The duke stared at her angel face with gloomy thoughtfulness for nearly a minute. She found it somewhat discomfitting. Then he said gloomily:

"Very well: I'll come in and wait."

He walked with a determined air down the passage into the sitting-room.

Pollyooly ran up to the attic to assure herself that the Lump was not in mischief—it was the last thing in the world that placid, but red-headed cherub was likely to get into; none the less she was always making sure of it. Then she came down to the kitchen, and set about cutting thin bread and butter for two persons.

As she cut it she wondered uneasily what had brought the duke to the King's Bench Walk. If there was one person in the world with regard to whom she did not enjoy a clear conscience, it was the duke.

Had he come for the reason:

(1) That she had helped the duchess in the original evasion of his daughter?

(2) That she had spent a fortnight at Ricksborough Court as his daughter?

(3) Or had he discovered that she had helped the duchess in the second evasion of Lady Marion?

(4) Had Mr. Wilkinson revealed how she had tricked him and the detective?

Truly there were reasons why she should be afflicted by an uneasy conscience with regard to the duke. It was no wonder that his gloomy stare had made her uncomfortable. She tried to reassure herself by the consideration that if he had discovered anything, he would surely have been far grumpier with her; he would never have confined himself to a gloomy stare.

She had just finished cutting the bread and butter when the latchkey of the Honourable John Ruffin grated in the keyhole.

She stepped to the kitchen door; and as he entered she said:

"Please, sir, the duke's here."

The Honourable John Ruffin showed no surprise; he only said:

"Ah, he must be wanting me to do something for him. I told you that he would warm to me when he did."

"Yes, sir. But, please sir, he doesn't look very warm yet," said Pollyooly doubtfully.

"He never does. It runs in the family—the Osterley chill. Bring us some tea," said the Honourable John Ruffin lightly;

and he went down the passage.

He came into the sitting-room briskly, and found the duke sitting in an easy chair, with his silk hat thrust well back on his head, in a fashion which gave him a far from ducal, an even raffish air.

"How are you, Ruffin?" he said, with an amiable smile, but in a somewhat nervous and deprecatory tone.

"How are you, Osterley? Got over the sulks?" said the Honourable John Ruffin lightly.

"Sulks? I never sulk!" said the duke with some heat.

"What do you call them then?" said the Honourable John Ruffin with a good display of the liveliest most unaffected interest.

"I don't know what you're talking about!" said the duke coldly; but he flushed.

It is likely that the Honourable John Ruffin would have raised him to a considerable temperature on this matter; but the entrance of Pollyooly, bearing the tea-tray, closed the discussion of it. The Honourable John Ruffin poured out the tea and handed the bread and butter to the duke.

They ate some bread and butter and drank some tea; and then the duke said plaintively:

"This is jolly good tea. Why don't I ever get tea like this?"

"You ought to. You pay enough for it," said the Honourable John Ruffin in a tone which lacked sympathy.

"I do. I believe I employ every incompetent jackass in London," said the duke bitterly.

"And I expect you don't make any secret of your conviction at home," said the Honourable John Ruffin.

"I don't," said the duke firmly; then yet more plaintively he added: "Oh, it's a dog's life for a man trying to run places like Ricksborough House and the court on his own!"

"I expect it does try you a bit too high," said the Honourable John Ruffin.

"It would any man," said the duke with conviction.

The Honourable John Ruffin thought that a man of tact and amiability could probably do it quite easily; but he did not say so. He thought that such a statement might be inhospitable. They went on with their tea in silence, the duke frowning over his luckless lot.

Then the Honourable John Ruffin said in a distinctly patient and long-suffering tone:

"Well, what is it you want me to do for you this time?"

"I don't want you to do anything for me!" said the duke sharply.

"Then what have you come for?" said the Honourable John Ruffin in the same distinctly patient and long-suffering tone.

The duke hesitated; then he said:

"Well, I want you to help me. I've got an idea."

The Honourable John Ruffin looked skeptical, indeed, and he said a little wearily:

"*You* have? What is it?"

The duke cleared his throat, assumed a portentous air, and said:

"I tell you I'm getting devilish sick of this business—living by myself, without any family, and that sort of thing. And I've come to the conclusion that it's time Caroline and I were reconciled—"

"High time," said the Honourable John Ruffin readily.

"I'm fond of Caroline—in a way—"

"Your own way—an obscure, secret way," said the Honourable John Ruffin in a cheerful tone.

The duke scowled at him, but went on: "You don't know how contrary Caroline is—"

"How should I? I'm not married to her," said the Honourable John Ruffin patiently.

"Well, she is. And I've been thinking that if she found she was getting her way without interference, she wouldn't want it any longer."

The keen grey eyes of the Honourable John Ruffin sparkled:

"By Jove! This is subtlety! Marriage makes Machiavellis of us all. Continue, Solomon," he said, with more respect in his tone.

"But I couldn't think of any way of letting her know she was getting it. It's no use writin' to those scoundrels of lawyers of hers and telling them. She'd only think it was a trap; or she'd think I'd caved in, and be so cockahoop we should never get any forrader. Then I got the idea. It looks a bit roundabout, but I believe it'll work, I do really. But it'll take a lot of working, and I'm wondering whether that little housekeeper of yours—what's her name—Mary Bride—will be up to it."

"What on earth has Pollyooly got to do with it?" cried the Honourable John Ruffin.

"A lot," said the duke firmly. "You know how like Marion she is. Why, even Mrs. Hutton, who'd been with Marion for years, couldn't tell them apart. Well, I want Mary Bride to be Marion."

"The deuce you do!" cried the Honourable John Ruffin.

"Yes," said the duke in the tone of a man who had quite made up his mind. "I want her to come and live at the court as Marion. I'm going to run her as my daughter, Lady Marion Ricksborough."

"But what on earth for?" cried the Honourable John Ruffin in a tone of the liveliest bewilderment.

"Why, don't you see? At first Caroline will be awfully cockahoop at getting her own way. Then she'll begin to see that Marion's out in the cold, and I've got another daughter in her place. Then she'll kick like fury. She'll send Marion back in a brace of shakes to take her proper place. Then it'll be my turn to kick. I shan't be taking any Marion—at least, not without Caroline comes back too," said the duke with an air of uncommon animation.

He was looking brighter than ever the Honourable John Ruffin had seen him. His eyes were positively gleaming with a manly fire.

"By Jove—by *Jove*!" said the Honourable John Ruffin softly.

"I thought you'd see it," said the duke complacently.

The Honourable John Ruffin rose from his chair, strode solemnly across the hearthrug, seized the duke's hand, wrung it, and in a voice trembling with emotion said:

"Osterley, I have done you an injustice. I have underrated your intellect. Under that mild and irritated appearance you hide genius—veritable genius. The idea is, as you say, roundabout, but it will work. It will certainly work. You are dealing with a woman."

The duke smiled with an air of the deepest self-satisfaction. Compliments from the Honourable John Ruffin were indeed rare.

"Yes; that's what I thought," he said. Then he chuckled, and added:

"Won't Caroline be mad when she finds I'm running another Marion?"

"'Mad' isn't the word for it," said the Honourable John Ruffin with conviction.

"I shall certainly be getting a little of my own back," said the duke, beaming.

The Honourable John Ruffin frowned at him heavily and said in a tone of the coldest severity:

"That's a stupid way of looking at it. The important thing about your idea is that it will very likely bring you together again. But I wonder if you can work it. You won't find it an easy job."

"It all depends on whether Mary Bride can take Marion's place," said the duke somewhat anxiously.

The Honourable John Ruffin looked at him queerly. It was not for him to say that Pollyooly had already spent a fortnight at Ricksborough Court as Lady Marion and that during that fortnight the duke had been as completely duped as his household.

He only said:

"It isn't Pollyooly I'm doubtful about. You need have no fears about her. She's by far the cleverest child I know, and she'll play her part all right. But, unfortunately, when you kidnapped her in Piccadilly and took her to Ricksborough House, your butler and Marion's nurse—what's her name?— Mrs. Hutton, learnt that Marion has a double, and they may suspect things."

"Oh, no: Lucas doesn't go to the court; and I discharged Mrs. Hutton for being an idiot. Also, I dismissed Miss Marlow, Marion's governess. I had no use for her. Really there's no one at the court now who came into close contact with Marion at all," said the duke.

"That does simplify things," said the Honourable John Ruffin cheerfully. "But of course it's going to be a matter of weeks. Caroline won't hear about it at once probably, for her friends won't hear about it to let her know. Then it'll take her some time to get over her satisfaction at having got her way, and to realise that Marion is out in the cold."

"Then she'll come back like a knife," said the duke.

"Yes; but Pollyooly has got to keep the game going for a good six weeks. Let's hear what she thinks about taking it on," said the Honourable John Ruffin, and he rang the bell.

"Of course she'll take it on. Besides having her at the court, I shall pay her a trifle," said the duke in a tone of complete assurance.

"You won't. You'll pay her at least five pounds a week," said the Honourable John Ruffin in an equally assured tone. "But even so, she may refuse to leave her little brother for so long."

CHAPTER XVIII

THE DUKE'S IDEA TAKES FORM

Pollyooly came quickly, but she came in some trepidation lest after all the duke might be going to scold her. A glance at his face reassured her: he was certainly not angry.

The Honourable John Ruffin said gravely:

"The duke wants you to do a piece of work for him, Pollyooly—a very well-paid piece of work."

At the words "well-paid" the duke started in his chair with a look of pain; but Pollyooly's deep blue eyes shone suddenly like bright stars, and she smiled a heavenly smile. It was not that she was mercenary. But it was the chief aim of her life to raise a wall of gold (it could not be too thick or too high) between the Lump and the workhouse.

"Yes?" she said a little breathlessly.

"He wants you to go down to his house in the country and pretend to be his little daughter, Lady Marion Ricksborough. You're exactly like her, and if you pretend properly, no one will know you're not her. Do you think you could do it?" said the Honourable John Ruffin briskly.

Edgar Jepson

Pollyooly smiled again, and said confidently:

"Oh, yes. I'm sure I could."

"And the duke will pay you seven or eight pounds a week for six weeks—so that it will mean thirty-five or forty pounds," said the Honourable John Ruffin with the same business briskness.

Pollyooly smiled another heavenly smile, but the duke sprang to his feet with harried air and cried fiercely:

"Oh, hang it all! Draw it mild, Ruffin! Seven or eight pounds a week for a child like that! Oh, hang it! It's too stiff!"

"Not a bit of it!" said the Honourable John Ruffin with cold business incisiveness. "Pollyooly has the monopoly of the likeness of Marion, and she must be paid a monopoly price. Besides, this business has been costing you over a thousand a year; surely you can't kick at seven or eight pounds a week for six weeks, or so, to stop it for good and all. Why, as a monopoly price, seven or eight pounds a week isn't enough. We must make it ten—or, say, a hundred for the whole job."

"No, no; seven pounds a week!" cried the duke hastily.

The Honourable John Ruffin looked at him with an air of considerable disapproval, almost contemptuous, and said coldly:

"Well, you can't expect me to haggle—seven let it be."

He would have been very well content to get five pounds a week for Pollyooly; and she would have been overjoyed to get it. But he did not think it wise to show any pleasure at getting seven.

But during this discussion of terms Pollyooly's face had fallen; and its brightness was dimmed. Somewhat plaintively she said:

"But please, your Grace. If it's going to take six weeks what's to become of the Lump?"

"Yes: there's certainly the Lump to be considered," said the Honourable John Ruffin, frowning.

"I couldn't go away for six whole weeks and leave the Lump," said Pollyooly.

"And who, or what, is the Lump?" said the duke somewhat impatiently.

"The Lump's her little brother. She mothers him," explained the Honourable John Ruffin.

"Well, surely she can find some one to take charge of him for six weeks. I'm paying her enough," said the duke.

"Oh, no, your Grace. I couldn't let anybody but myself look after him for a whole six weeks. I couldn't really. I shouldn't feel that they would do it properly—all the time. I can't go away and leave him for six weeks," said Pollyooly; and it was plain enough that she was quite sincere in her aversion from doing so.

Indeed she spoke in a tone of unshakable resolution; and the Honourable John Ruffin and the duke gazed at one another nonplussed. Pollyooly gazed at the Honourable John Ruffin with expectant eyes; she had a great belief in his powers. But he only frowned, pondering; and the duke scratched his head.

Then she said in a tone of faint hopefulness:

Edgar Jepson

"But couldn't I take the Lump with me?"

"That's a solution," said the Honourable John Ruffin quickly.

"Oh, hang it! I couldn't turn up with two children. It would upset the apple-cart," the duke protested.

The face of the Honourable John Ruffin grew clear; and he said firmly:

"It looks the only solution; and after all why shouldn't you adopt the Lump? People do adopt children."

"Not dukes," said the duke coldly.

"Oh, if you break the ice, I expect they'll adopt them by the dozen," said the Honourable John Ruffin cheerfully. "There isn't any real reason why you shouldn't. You have this new and very proper desire to become thoroughly domesticated. The Lump is one of the very people to gratify it. Besides, it will give the people at the court something to talk about, and take their minds off Pollyooly."

"I should jolly well think it would!" growled the duke.

"Well, it's the only thing to do," said the Honourable John Ruffin.

"Do you think so?" said the duke doubtfully; and he blinked.

"I'm sure of it," said the Honourable John Ruffin confidently. "You can't have Pollyooly without the Lump."

The duke shook his head, turned to Pollyooly, and said:

"I tell you what: I'll make it eight pounds a week, if you'll come alone."

Pollyooly shook her head and said sadly:

"I couldn't, your Grace. I couldn't really."

It looked indeed like a blind alley; but in the end the duke yielded. His heart was set on carrying through this scheme for regaining his duchess. His mind was so rarely guilty of ingenuity that he could not bear to discourage it. They set themselves, therefore, to making the presence of the Lump at Ricksborough Court plausible. Fortunately he was too young to spoil their plan by indiscreet babble, had he been a babbling child. To the minds of the servants at Ricksborough Court, minds so carefully trained in the board schools of England, his pregnant grunts would convey no meaning.

Then arose the question of a becoming outfit; and into this matter the Honourable John Ruffin threw himself with enthusiasm. He saw his way to remove the burden of new summer clothes for herself and the Lump from Pollyooly's slender resources for several years.

More than once the duke protested that he was not taking the children to live at the court for the rest of the century; and when the Honourable John Ruffin thoughtfully tried to edge in a few winter vests, he protested hotly that he was not fitting out an expedition to discover the North Pole, or the South.

His warm opposition only excited the combative instinct of the Honourable John Ruffin. Coldly he urged the well-known inclemency of the English summer; surely the duke did not wish to have two pneumonic children on his hands; and the vests slipped into the outfit.

Edgar Jepson

The duke was resolved to give the affair the strongest possible air of verisimilitude; and he engaged a governess, a Miss Belthrop, for Pollyooly. That led to his engaging a nurse, Emily Gibbs, for the Lump, though Pollyooly protested that it was quite unnecessary.

The duke was indeed falling more and more deeply in love with his scheme the nearer it came to putting it into effect. On three afternoons he came to coach Pollyooly in the topography of Ricksborough Court and its gardens, and in the habits of Lady Marion Ricksborough. He was astonished and impressed by her intelligence. He was called on to tell her hardly a single thing twice. He spoke of it to the Honourable John Ruffin with great respect.

Then on the tenth day after his first visit he came in a taxicab, greatly excited, for them and their luggage, and drove them to Waterloo Station. On the platform they found Emily Gibbs, in charge of Lawrence, the duke's valet, awaiting them. She found favour in the exigent eyes of Pollyooly, who let her take charge of the Lump without a single anxious qualm. Emily Gibbs fell in love with him at first sight.

Pollyooly, though all the while she kept a careful eye on him, left him in the care of Emily Gibbs, till the train was actually outside London. Then she took him into her corner and pointed out objects of interest to him. She was convinced that he had made a great advance in intelligence since his journey down to Pyechurch: not once did he hail a sheep as a gee-gee. She promoted him to the use of his proper Christian name, and called him Roger. The duke had grown calm once more, and read a four-penny-half-penny magazine with every appearance of absorbed interest.

In the motor car which carried them from Ricksborough station to the court, Pollyooly insisted on having the Lump on her knee. Motor drives did not come their way so often that she could bear to be parted from him in an hour of such delight.

Once out of the peaceful seclusion of the railway carriage the duke's excitement had returned; and now that the real ordeal was at hand, he had grown uncommonly nervous. It may be that he was unused to deceit. He had set Emily Gibbs beside the chauffeur that he might have Pollyooly to himself; and all the way he poured jumbled instructions into her ear in a fashion which would have brought her to the court hopelessly confused had she been paying much attention to him. As she followed him up the steps of the court she fancied that he was even shaky on his legs.

Rawlings, the butler, greeted them with a cold and dignified civility which showed him thoroughly aware of his own value. Also there was a lack of geniality in his tone which showed that he did not greatly love the duke; and the one smile he lavished on Pollyooly was stiff and wooden. But she certainly passed his careless scrutiny.

Then, they had gone but a few steps into the hall when a slim and serpentine dachshund trotted forward to greet them. It avoided the duke and sniffed at Pollyooly. Then it uttered a yelp of joy, and began to dance round her. At the yelp, four more small dogs hurried down the hall, and flung themselves on Pollyooly with every sign of the warmest affection.

The duke gasped and blinked, suddenly assumed a Machiavellian air, and said, for the benefit of the butler and footman, in a high, unnatural voice:

"Well, at any rate, the dogs haven't forgotten you, Marion."

"No, papa," said Pollyooly with an angel smile.

CHAPTER XIX

POLLYOOLY IS INTRODUCED
TO THE COUNTY

He had never done it before, but to-day, to the surprise of his butler, the duke accompanied his supposed daughter up the stairs to Lady Marion Ricksborough's suite of rooms. His face was flushed; and he stumbled twice. His mind was full of the strange behaviour of the serpentine dachshund and the other dogs.

When they had risen above the range of hearing of the butler and footmen in the hall, he said somewhat breathlessly:

"I was never so flabbergasted in my life. Fancy dogs taking to you like that! When I saw Hildegarde, who is one of the most particular dogs I ever came across, dancing round you like that, you could have knocked me down with a feather."

"Yes: it is funny," said Pollyooly; and she smiled.

"But what a blessing it is!" the duke went on quickly. "It will be all over the place that the dogs recognised you; and after that it's no good whatever any one's saying that you're not Marion. It settles it—absolutely."

"I suppose it does," said Pollyooly calmly.

She had no intention in the world of telling him that the dogs had the best of reasons for recognising her, in that they actually had known her before. It did not trouble her at all to leave him in error. It suited his purpose so well that no one should know that she had ever been at the court before.

The suite of rooms when Pollyooly had last occupied it, had consisted of her bedroom and school-room, and the bedroom and the sitting-room of the governess. To these the duke had added a nursery bedroom for the Lump and a bedroom for his nurse.

In the schoolroom they found Miss Belthorp awaiting them; and the duke presented her to Pollyooly. Then with the air of an operating Camorrist he showed Pollyooly which was her bedroom by the crafty device of pretending to make sure that her sheets had been aired.

Pollyooly at once demanded that the Lump should also sleep in it. It seemed a very natural desire on the part of a little girl; and, much to the disgust of Emily Gibbs, who wished to have him to herself as much as possible, the duke ordered a cot to be brought into it.

Then with the same Machiavellian air, he said to Miss Belthorp:

"Lady Marion has taken a strong fancy to this little boy I'm adopting. I hope it will last."

"It's sure to, your Grace. He's such a dear little boy," said Miss Belthorp with conviction, for she, too, had fallen a victim to the silent charm of the Lump.

Having done his best to secure the first success of his plan, the duke left them. Pollyooly made haste to have their trunk unpacked; and then, having put on a linen frock, while Emily Gibbs put one on the Lump, she took him out into the gardens. Miss Belthorp accompanied them; and it seemed to Pollyooly that she was uncommonly like Miss Marlow, Lady Marion's earlier governess, whom she had found at the court during her last stay there. She realised very soon that it was really unnecessary to listen to her conversation; the chance of her saying anything of any real interest being so very small.

From the windows of the smoking-room the duke saw the two children crossing the terrace, accompanied by a large proportion of the dogs of the establishment. In his glowing self-satisfaction with the success of the first part of his plan, he found that they greatly improved the appearance of the gardens.

The Lump approved greatly of the gardens; but he was a little doubtful about the dogs, and kept a firm hold of Pollyooly's skirts. It was nearly ten minutes before, encouraged by the very friendly way in which Pollyooly treated them, he really unbent. He showed a truly marvellous instinct for discovering which dog would let him pull his tail, and which would not.

Pollyooly thought it wise to relax a little from her usual exact mothering of him. She had him sit by her at tea of course; but she let Emily Gibbs give him his bath, and contented herself with watching the operation. She was pleased that the Lump did not accept the change without objection. He pointed to her and said quite severely:

"Pollyooly."

"It's all right, Roger dear," she said in a soothing tone. Then turning to Emily Gibbs, she added: "I wonder what he means?"

"I don't know, your ladyship. But he is the dearest little boy I ever see!" said Emily Gibbs with enthusiasm. "I never knew as how there was such a little boy!" and she kissed him.

Pollyooly frowned slightly. These transports seemed to her misplaced. They were an invasion of her proprietary rights in him. But she did not frown long: after all, the fonder Emily Gibbs was of him the more carefully she would watch over him.

At supper in the servants' hall Emily Gibbs underwent a severe cross-examination. The coming of the Lump to the court had indeed set tongues wagging; and Rawlings, since he had failed to find the duke quite satisfactory, was doing nothing to check it. The chief housemaid and the second cook (the *chef* was a Frenchman with a strong Italian accent which marked also his cooking) seemed to have made up their minds that Emily Gibbs must necessarily have been made the repository of the secret of the Lump's origin; and they spared no effort to extract that secret from her. Emily Gibbs had the most uncomfortable supper of her life: her fellow-servants, naturally, resented bitterly the fact that she had met the Lump for the first time that very day at Waterloo station. They wanted pegs on which to hang romance; and she did not provide them.

At last the second cook said:

"Well: it's as plain as a pikestaff to me that that little boy is the son of a young lady as his grace was in love with before he ever met the duchess. And she married somebody else; and they're both dead; and his grace 'as adopted their little

Edgar Jepson

boy for old sake's sake."

The first housemaid and the second housemaid accepted this theory warmly; and then Emily Gibbs said:

"And I expect she had red hair."

The basic facts of the affair having been thus comfortably settled, the talk turned on the identity of the lady, and then on the colour of her hair. Rawlings was of the opinion that the redness of the Lump's hair was evidence that either his father or his mother had been a relation of the duke, since there was so much red hair in the Osterley family. His suggestion met with general approval.

"It certainly makes his adopting him more natural-like," said the second housemaid.

Pollyooly was awake the next morning before any one else at the court; and soon after six she rose. She dressed the Lump, gave him biscuits, ate some herself; and accompanied by all the loose dogs in the house, they went out into the gardens through one of the long windows of the blue drawing-room. She led the Lump round to the stables and there unloosed several more dogs, so that they went about the world well attended, and spent two very pleasant hours before their exigent appetites demanded their return to breakfast.

The duke saw them returning from his dressing-room; and once more he was of the opinion that they improved the appearance of the gardens.

As it was Lady Marion's first day at the court after so many months, Miss Belthorp decided that it should be a holiday—a holiday for Pollyooly, that is; the Lump did not appear to be yet ripe to learn even the alphabet.

After breakfast therefore they went out again; and Miss Belthorp went with them. This was of no advantage to them, for the excursion became a formal walk, much less attractive than their erratic wanderings when alone. Also it was a walk along paths; there were no incursions into the heart of the woods they went through, nor did they go in a single meadow and roll in the grass with the dogs. Also, since the hour was undeniably shining, she thought it well to improve it by imparting a little instruction in botany. Pollyooly found it quite uninteresting; she did not care at all whether a flower had four stems or fourteen. Stamens seemed to her childish mind quite unimportant; the colour and fragrance of the flower seemed to her the only important things.

As they came into the court Miss Belthorp chanced to say:

"I do hope that you haven't been neglecting your piano, Marion. I always think that music is so important in the formation of character."

Pollyooly had not been neglecting her piano, because she had no piano to neglect. The piano played no part in any of the seven standards she had passed at Muttle Deeping school; and she did not know one note from another. She was taken aback by the suggestion that she was expected to show herself accomplished in music. Evidently she must consult the duke.

She and the Lump and Miss Belthorp lunched with him, or rather they dined and he lunched. After it, having seen the Lump safely on his way upstairs with Miss Belthorp, Pollyooly followed the duke into the smoking-room.

"Please, your Grace: Miss Belthorp seems to expect me to know how to play the piano; and I don't know how to at all," she said gravely.

"The deuce you don't!" said the duke. "Here's another thing I never thought of."

"I don't *mind* learning the piano," said Pollyooly with a sigh.

"Yes; but if you showed that you didn't know anything about it, it would look very suspicious indeed," said the duke; and he frowned deeply as he cudgelled his brains for a way out of this unexpected difficulty.

"I expect it would," said Pollyooly.

He frowned on, fidgeting; then he said with decision:

"Well, the only thing to do is to stop it altogether."

"That would be quite safe," said Pollyooly brightening.

"All right: I'll see to it," said the duke.

Pollyooly left him with her heart at ease.

He frowned over the matter for some time, for it did not seem to him to be quite in the natural order of things that a duke should actually refuse to allow his daughter to learn the piano. But he could find no other way of concealing Pollyooly's damning ignorance of the art of music.

At last therefore he sent for Miss Belthorp and said:

"I—er—have decided that—er—Poll—er—Lady Marion is not to learn the piano."

"Not learn the piano?" said Miss Belthorp in the tone of one afflicted with the last amazement.

"I—er—have never observed the—er—slightest aptitude in her for it," said the duke with perfect truthfulness.

Miss Belthorp blinked. She prided herself on the brilliancy with which she played the piano—especially the scherzo passages.

"But—b—but she looks such an intelligent child," she said.

"Yes. That's why," said the duke happily.

Miss Belthorp blinked again; then in a somewhat helpless tone she said:

"Oh, very well, your Grace."

When the door closed behind her, the duke smiled happily and rubbed his hands together.

Pollyooly was expecting to spend a quiet afternoon in the gardens and home wood with the Lump and the dogs and perhaps Miss Belthorp. She hoped that Miss Belthorp would have some more important way of spending her time. Of Emily Gibbs she could easily dispose, since already she was giving her orders with a quiet firmness there was no gainsaying. Indeed, Emily Gibbs had been far too well brought up not to receive orders from what she called "A Lady of Title," with humble gratitude, and execute them with vigour and despatch; and already she was hard at work making linen overalls for the Lump. But at half-past three, just as Miss Belthorp had left them to write letters and they had started for the home wood, the obedient Emily came hurrying along the garden to say that the duke wished Pollyooly to put on her prettiest clothes and come with him to pay a call.

Pollyooly frowned deeply at the thought that had not Miss Belthorp lingered with them, they would by now have been safely hidden in some recess of the wood. For the moment she almost wished that the Lump were not so attractive. But very soon she was serene again. After all it was a pleasant thing to be prettily dressed and ride in a motor car; and there was always the exciting anticipation that the cakes at tea would not only be delicious but quite uncommon.

She dressed therefore in a complete serenity and gave Emily Gibbs careful and exact instructions about the care of the Lump during her absence. Then a footman came up to say that the car was ready; and she went down the stairs comfortably assured that she was looking her prettiest. She saw that the duke looked pleased at the sight of her; his face grew quite bright.

He put her into the tonneau of the car and stepped in after her. It was not the first time they had been alone together, but for the moment she felt somewhat oppressed. But he at once began to instruct her in the manners and deportment in vogue at garden parties; and presently she was talking to him with the most amiable affability.

Three-quarters of an hour's drive brought them to Ilkeston Towers, their destination; and when Pollyooly and the duke, coming on to the lawn, which was set with groups of brightly dressed, shrilly chattering people, were loudly announced by a strong-lunged butler, there was a sudden hush and a general, quickly checked movement toward them. Then Lady Ilkeston greeted them; and the duke said to her in a somewhat loud voice:

"It's rather dull going about alone, so I brought Marion with me."

"But how nice!" said Lady Ilkeston; and she welcomed Pollyooly warmly.

There was by no means an immediate rush to make Pollyooly's acquaintance; but for half an hour Lady Ilkeston found herself busy introducing to her people who were firmly resolved to make her acquaintance, since she was, so to speak, the sub-heroine of the most interesting local scandal.

The duke had not looked for anything of the kind; and he was on tenterhooks; he had expected that as a child she would be left peacefully in the background. He found her the central figure of the gathering; and he was in the liveliest dread lest she should fail to come through the ordeal with her secret safe.

It never for a moment occurred to Pollyooly that her secret was in any danger. Naturally therefore she wore an air of perfect ease; and answered the innumerable questions about her fondness for different things, the country, dolls, flowers and so forth with serene simplicity. He was somewhat surprised by her air (it was not accentuated, or even obvious) of faintly haughty aloofness. He had a feeling that it was exactly the right air for a daughter of a duke. He wondered how it had come to her, whether the Honourable John Ruffin was right in his red Deeping theory. He did not know his experienced cousin had often laid before Pollyooly the advantage of giving herself airs, and she had not been slow to see it. He grew easier in mind.

Lady Ilkeston was the person really pleased. She had not expected to have any really interesting central figure at her afternoon; and she was all the more grateful at getting one. Her gratitude took the practical form of instructing Sir Miles Walpole, an amiable young man of twenty-four, very fond of

Edgar Jepson

children, to take Pollyooly to the long table under the cedars, and give her a very nice tea indeed. The ices and the cakes, which surpassed her hopes and expectation, to no small degree compensated Pollyooly for the loss of that untrammelled ramble through the home wood. Also she enjoyed the society of Sir Miles Walpole; she was at once thoroughly at home with him.

Soon after tea the duke took her away. When the car had started, he said triumphantly:

"Well, we came through that all right. Not a soul spotted that you weren't Marion."

"But how could they?" said Pollyooly in a tone of lively surprise.

"Oh, I was a bit afraid at first," said the duke.

"I wasn't," said Pollyooly simply.

He took off his hat, let the rushing air cool his brow, and smiled broadly at the horizon. It seemed to him that if Pollyooly were the central figure in yet another gathering, or two, the duchess would not be long in hearing that he had with uncommon success replaced his lost daughter.

CHAPTER XX

POLLYOOLY AND THE DUKE

The duke's delight with the evident publicity which had attended the presentation of Pollyooly to the county had lessened hardly at all by the next morning. He thought it likely that, if the duchess were anywhere in the United Kingdom, she would learn by some post that very day that he had filled the place of Marion.

Then it occurred to him that these correspondents would not only condole with the duchess on having lost her daughter, but also they would condole with her on having lost such a charming and delightful daughter; and he laughed more heartily than he had laughed for many a long day.

In a natural desire for yet more publicity, that afternoon he took Pollyooly with him and drove over to Overton Grange to introduce her to the Ashcrofts, who had tried to play the part of mediators, with signal ill-success, between him and the duchess. The Ashcrofts had heard that Lady Marion Ricksborough had been present at the garden party at Ilkeston Towers the day before. They were surprised by the news and more than a little hurt that the duchess had not at once informed them that the duke had recovered her. Also they were feeling that the duke had brought Pollyooly to show her off to them as his triumph. Therefore Lord Ashcroft, a strong, silent, bearded man, was a trifle stiff with him, Lady Ashcroft a trifle cold; but they made up for it by giving Pollyooly the warmest welcome possible; their friend-liness was almost overwhelming. After tea (to Pollyooly's regret there were no ices) Lady Ashcroft took her up to the nurseries where she found a little girl of eight and a little boy of six, and enjoyed herself thoroughly. They were better than ices.

Lord Ashcroft and the duke smoked their cigarettes in silence for a while after Lady Ashcroft and Pollyooly had left them. Lord Ashcroft looked rather gloomy; the duke looked at peace with the world. Then Lord Ashcroft said gloomily:

"How did you get hold of Marion?"

"Oh, money—just money," said the duke airily but with perfect truthfulness.

Lord Ashcroft frowned; and they were silent again.

The duke, with the same air of content, lighted another cigarette.

Presently Lord Ashcroft said:

"She's very much improved both in looks and intelligence."

The duke sat bolt upright and said quickly and with heat:

"She's nothing of the kind!"

"Oh, yes; she is. You know she is," said Lord Ashcroft firmly. "It's being with her mother."

"It's nothing of the kind!" said the duke, still with heat. It seemed to him absurd to suggest that Pollyooly was superior to his daughter.

"It is; and I shall write and tell Caroline so," said Lord Ashcroft with the same firmness.

"I never knew such an obstinate—wrong-headed—" the duke broke out. He broke off short, paused, began to laugh, and laughed heartily. Then he said: "Oh, well; have it your own way. Write and tell her so."

"I shall," said Lord Ashcroft in the tone of one bent on performing a sacred duty. "I don't see anything to laugh at."

The duke again remained silent; but twice he laughed sudden, short laughs. Lord Ashcroft looked at him suspiciously.

"I don't know quite what's happening to you, Osterley," he said presently in a tone hardly meant to be pleasant. "You're changing."

"Yes: getting brighter," said the duke easily.

"It may be that and again it may not," said Lord Ashcroft coldly; and he tugged at his beard.

After that conversation seemed hard to make; and soon the duke said that he must be going. Lady Ashcroft kept him waiting nearly twenty minutes before she brought Pollyooly down from the nurseries. Then she said that Pollyooly must come to spend the whole day with her children; and Pollyooly said that she would like to come very much. The duke looked a little doubtful: he was not sure that Pollyooly could stand the test of hours of intimacy.

Edgar Jepson

On the way home he talked for a while cheerfully; and since there was no intellectual gulf between them, they could talk to one another with perfect ease and understanding. Then he fell into a sudden panic.

"By Jove!" he cried, clutching at his moustache and missing it. "I'd forgotten all about it! My sister—Lady Salkeld's coming home to-morrow!"

Pollyooly said nothing. She looked at him with enquiring eyes.

"Suppose she goes and recognises that you aren't Marion?"

"I don't see why she should any more than any one else," said Pollyooly in a reassuring tone.

"Oh, but, hang it! She's seen a lot of Marion. She's known her ever since she was a baby," said the duke with a harassed air.

Pollyooly could have set his mind at rest by assuring him that during her last stay at the court Lady Salkeld had not shown the slightest tendency to recognise that she was not Lady Marion Ricksborough; but she did not. She only said:

"I don't suppose that she'll take much notice of me."

"There is that. She pretty well thinks of nothing but her own affairs," said the duke more hopefully.

"Anyhow, it's no use worrying about it. I expect it'll be all right," said Pollyooly in a comforting tone.

The duke was so far reassured by her careless serenity as presently to resume his easy conversation with her. That evening, since he was dining alone, he sent for her to come to him at dessert, and talked to her again. His was a sociable nature; and in view of the presence of her and the Lump he had not invited any friends to relieve the loneliness of his stay at the court.

Lady Salkeld arrived in time for lunch next day; and at lunch Pollyooly and the Lump met her. The duke was on tenter-hooks, needlessly, for she bestowed a tepid kiss on Pollyooly, tapped the cheek of the Lump even more tepidly, and addressed herself peaceably to her lunch.

But after a while she began to give her attention to the Lump, looking at him earnestly now and again, and blinking. Then she said:

"That child reminds me of somebody, Osterley. Where did you pick him up?"

"These red Deepings are all alike," said the duke carelessly.

"Oh? He's a red Deeping, is he? Who's his father?" said Lady Salkeld almost briskly.

"It's a secret," said the duke with perfect truthfulness, for he did not know.

Lady Salkeld looked at him, sniffed, and said with some tartness:

"Well, I never expected you to be mysterious, Osterley."

The duke bore the reproach with patient meekness, and said nothing. It suited him very well that his sister should be giving her attention to the Lump. From the Lump nothing was to be learned.

Lady Salkeld's coming made no difference to their lives. Pollyooly went on her early morning rambles with the Lump; from breakfast to noon she did her lessons and then went for a sedate walk with Miss Belthorp. After lunch she played with the Lump till it was time to drive out to tea with the duke. Naturally she met the same people again and again, and was now on very friendly terms with some of them. The duke, regarding her with something of the feeling of an impresario, and finding that she was everywhere welcomed as an authentic angel child, began to take pride in displaying her. Also he began to take greater pleasure in her society. Frequently, when the morning lessons were over, he would come up to the schoolroom and take her out for a walk with him. He liked to stroll about his estate and thrill with the feelings of a landed proprietor.

Pollyooly enjoyed these walks. The duke never tried to improve her mind with botany. But she learned much country lore from him, the names and habits of many birds and small animals. In spite of his exalted station, he was a simple soul; and he had retained his boyish interest in the furred and feathered world of the woods and meadows round the court. Also he enjoyed telling Pollyooly things. Unconsciously, but quite accurately, he regarded her as his intellectual equal; and it pleased him very much to tell her things she did not know. It gave him a sense of passing, but genuine superiority, a feeling his fellow creatures seldom inspired into him.

Sometimes he wondered why he had never thought of making a companion of Marion. He made up his mind that when, presently, he was reconciled with the duchess (he had no doubt ever that presently they would be reconciled) he would make a companion of her. It never entered his mind that there would be any difficulty about doing so.

The Honourable John Ruffin came down for a week-end and was pleased to find the duke and Pollyooly on such excellent terms. So pleased was he that he forebore, by a considerable effort, to tease the duke. At least he did not tease him more than was good for him. Also, to his great surprise, he found himself suffering from a twinge of jealousy now and again at Pollyooly's frank display of friendliness for the duke. He told himself that it was wholly absurd. But there it was: with his money and influence the duke could do so much more for her than he could. He consoled himself with the thought that after all the duke would be only carrying on his work.

On the Saturday afternoon they went, as was their wont, for a stroll through the woods; and the Honourable John Ruffin, who had so carefully gratified his great inborn interest in the human race that now he missed very little, observed that once or twice the duke paused and looked about him as if he missed something.

The next afternoon as they were starting, the duke said in a voice which was not as easy as it tried to be, and with an air that was distinctly shame-faced:

"I say: we may as well take Pollyooly with us."

The Honourable John Ruffin raised his eyebrows a little and said:

"Oh, well—little pitchers have long ears, don't you know."

"Oh, that's all right—that's all right, we needn't talk secrets," said the duke quickly; and he ran lightly up the stairs to fetch her.

It was a pleasant walk; and the Honourable John Ruffin was alive to the fact that the company of Pollyooly greatly

Edgar Jepson

improved it. But at times to his astonishment he was no less distinctly conscious of the fact that two were company and three were none; and he was the third.

At dinner that night he said somewhat gloomily:

"I wish Caroline would hurry up and start firmly to come back to you. I miss Pollyooly."

"Give her time—give her time," said the duke quickly. "Besides the country is doing the child a lot of good."

"Oh, it's all very well for you. You've got a chef; but I've got no one to grill my bacon, and that after training Pollyooly to be the finest griller of bacon in England," said the Honourable John Ruffin in a bitterly aggrieved tone.

"Don't you think you're a bit selfish? You ought to think of the good the country's doing the child," said the duke in a somewhat lofty tone.

The Honourable John Ruffin snarled quietly.

The next afternoon, as he was getting into the car to go to the station, he paused and said in his most amiable tone:

"Well, all I can say is: it's a jolly good thing for everybody that Pollyooly isn't six years older."

"Oh, get out!" said the duke.

"Especially for Pollyooly," said the Honourable John Ruffin; and he stepped into the car.

CHAPTER XXI

LORD RONALD RICKSBOROUGH
COMES TO THE COURT

On the Wednesday morning, in the middle of lessons, a footman came from the duke to ask Pollyooly to go to him at once. She went wondering, and found him in the smoking-room in a panic.

As she entered he waved a telegram at her and said:

"Here's a new mess. Lord Ronald Ricksborough—you know him—he's my heir, you know—always spends his holidays at the court. He's been visiting friends, but his visit's at an end; and he wires to say that he's coming here—arriving this evening."

"Oh, that will be nice!" cried Pollyooly.

"Oh, will it? Suppose he finds out you're not Lady Marion?" cried the duke.

"But he knows I'm not; and he knows I'm here," said Pollyooly.

"The deuce he does!" cried the duke.

Edgar Jepson

"Yes. I wrote and told him so," said Pollyooly.

"You did?" cried the duke; and he clutched at his moustache.

"Yes. We often write to one another—just short letters. You know we're engaged to be married, when we grow up. He gave me this ring," said Pollyooly in a tone of quiet explanation, holding out her hand.

The duke gasped heavily.

"I don't know what the world's coming to! Children of your age!" he cried.

"Oh, it'll be quite all right," said Pollyooly cheerfully. "I'm going on the stage. I've been on it already—dancing with the Esmeralda—not really dancing of course, but just filling in the picture (that's what the Esmeralda called it) in 'Titania's Awakening'—"

"What? You were the child in 'Titania's Awakening'?" said the duke heavily.

"Yes. But when I grow up I'm going on the stage again—in musical comedy—so that it will be quite all right for Ronald to marry me. The heirs of peers generally marry girls in musical comedy. Ronald says they do; and Mr. Ruffin said that he was quite right."

The duke's eyes were larger than usual, and bulging out. He ground his teeth and looked as if he could well have torn out some of his hair.

"I can't think why John Ruffin will talk such silly nonsense!" he growled in a tone of the last exasperation.

"Oh, but it isn't, your Grace," said Pollyooly reproachfully. "Lots of them have done it. Ronald sent me a list of them he made out with two school-fellows. Only it's at the Temple. It'll be quite all right for us to get married."

The duke gnashed his teeth for a change. But he regained some control of himself and said with moderate calmness:

"Well, of course it's only children's nonsense. But you may as well bear in mind that Ronald's going to marry Lady Marion."

"I don't think you'll get him to," said Pollyooly quickly but dispassionately. "He says she's such a little duff—" Her natural politeness stopped the word on her tongue. "They—they don't get on well together."

"They'll have to!" said the duke stormily.

Pollyooly said nothing; but she did not look hopeful.

The duke waited for a word of encouragement. It did not come. He crumpled up the telegram, threw it into the grate, and said:

"But the real question is: will Ronald keep the secret? Will he be able to?"

"Oh, yes: he'll keep it quite easily," said Pollyooly confidently. "He's splendid at keeping secrets."

The duke gazed at her gloomily and said gloomily:

"I can't conceive how on earth you and Ronald got to know one another so well."

Pollyooly's eyes opened wider and grew uncommonly limpid. She said:

"Oh, I've been out to lunch with him and to the Varolium—from the Temple."

"You have, have you?" said the duke bitterly. "I'm hanged if I know what the world's coming to!"

Pollyooly said nothing. She looked at him solemnly as if impressed by his difficulty. He gazed at her gloomily. Then he said firmly:

"Look here: I'm not going to have his coming interfere with our walks; and he's not coming with us to call on people."

Pollyooly knitted her brow and after a thoughtful pause said:

"I shouldn't think he'll want to."

"He won't, if he does," said the duke firmly. "And mind you keep him up to the mark and see that he doesn't let out that you're not Marion."

"Oh, I will," said Pollyooly.

"Well, run away and get your lessons done. I hope to goodness he doesn't let it out!"

That evening, while they were at tea, Lord Ronald Ricksborough arrived, and came straight to the schoolroom. His attitude was admirable. He greeted Pollyooly with the words, "Hullo, Marion!" in the perfectly perfunctory manner of a cousin. She greeted him with a like perfunctoriness and introduced him to Miss Belthorp. He greeted her politely; then he looked at the Lump with a very good air of surprise and said:

"Who's the kid?"

This display of ignorance was unwarranted by the fact that more than once, in moments of chivalry, he had carried the Lump up the stairs of Seventy-five, the King's Bench Walk, after the three of them had been taking their pleasures in London.

"He's a little boy his grace has adopted," said Miss Belthorp, smiling affectionately at the Lump.

"Adopted? Well, that's a rum go," said Ronald; and he sat down at the table.

Over his tea he told them, or, to be exact, he told Pollyooly, for it was to her that he addressed himself, of his doings at school and during the time he had spent on the visit which had just come to an end. After tea he and Pollyooly went out into the gardens together. When they were out of hearing he said:

"This is tophole, having you here, old girl!"

Then as they passed out of sight in a shrubbery, he put his arm, somewhat clumsily for one in most things uncommonly deft, round her neck and kissed her. Pollyooly returned the kiss in a matter-of-fact, almost careless fashion. She was not addicted to kissing, though she kissed the Lump often enough and with fervour; but this kiss was part of the business of being engaged to be married. Since Ronald heaved a sigh of relief at having performed the required feat, it is to be presumed that his feelings in the matter were very like her own. Then they went on briskly through the gardens and into the wood, the best companions in the world.

With Ronald at the court the days grew pleasanter than ever. He begged Pollyooly to demand that she too should have a holiday. But this she would not do. She had seen the world at too close quarters to throw away things idly; and she was learning French. Indeed, the lessons had been reduced to French because Pollyooly had heard the Esmeralda say that she found her knowledge of French a perfect blessing; and agreeing with her, the Honourable John Ruffin had said that to an artist who danced on the continent and in the Americas, French must be worth hundreds a year.

Pollyooly had the firmest intention of dancing herself on the continent and in the Americas, and she applied herself to learning the French tongue with the vigour and tenacity with which she worked at her dancing. Miss Belthorp was astonished at the quickness with which she learnt; and she talked with enthusiasm to the duke of his daughter's gift for languages.

"She has: has she?" said the duke; and he looked at her somewhat queerly.

"It's perfectly wonderful!" said Miss Belthorp.

"Oh, well: it's a very good thing. I dare say it will come in useful one of these days," said the duke.

On their walk that morning he told Pollyooly that Miss Belthorp had said that she was a marvel at languages; and Pollyooly was very pleased to hear it. She told the duke her reason for working so hard at her French.

He frowned for the next hundred yards, or so; then he said irritably:

"I can't see why on earth you want to go in for this dancing and all this stage business at all."

"Oh, but if you can dance—really dance, they pay you ever so well," cried Pollyooly.

"I tell you what it is: you're a jolly sight too keen on money—for a child of your age—it's—it's mercenary—yes: mercenary," said the duke severely.

Pollyooly flushed, and looked at him with her eyes bright either with tears, or a sparkle of anger.

"But I *have* to get money," she said with some heat. "When Mr. Ruffin's creditors hale him away to the deepest dungeon in Holloway (he's said they will lots of times) you don't suppose I'm going to let the Lump go to the workhouse! And where should I get another place like Mr. Ruffin's? I should only have Mr. Gedge-Tomkins."

"Oh, well—of course—if it's like that," said the duke in a tone of awkward apology.

Pollyooly said nothing for a while; she walked on with knitted brow. Then she said:

"And anyhow when the Lump gets bigger, I shall want a lot of money. There'll be his clothes, and his schooling. I don't want him to go to a board school—not in London. Such children go there—Aunt Hannah said so, and so does Mrs. Brown. But there must be schools where they wouldn't charge very much."

"Oh—ah—of course, you'll want money for that," said the duke heavily.

Pollyooly gave a little skip as of one removing an unpleasant matter from her mind, and said cheerfully:

"And anyhow I should have to go on the stage. Ronald and I couldn't get married if I didn't."

"I keep telling you that he's going to marry Marion," said the duke very firmly indeed.

His insistence on this fact did not seem to impair Pollyooly's cheerful serenity, for after a thoughtful pause she skipped again and said:

"Oh, well: if I'm actually on the stage, I expect it would be all right. There must be other heirs of peers."

The duke looked down on her and said bitterly:

"I'm hanged if *I* know what the world's coming to!"

CHAPTER XXII

THE DUKE WINS

Pollyooly had been at Ricksborough Court rather more than a month when the Honourable John Ruffin arrived, uninvited and without notice, on the Friday evening. He found the duke in the garden with the three children.

"The kicking has begun," he said to the duke briefly, by way of explanation.

The duke seemed taken aback by the suddenness of the news, but soon he recovered and showed himself in very good spirits.

That night after dinner, after Pollyooly and Ronald had been dismissed from dessert to bed, the Honourable John Ruffin said:

"I got a letter from Caroline, pitching into me like one o'clock for being a party to a disgraceful plot to rob Marion of her name and birthright."

"Where is it?" said the duke quickly.

"I didn't bring it with me. The home-truths about me on it

were nothing to the home-truths about you. It would sear your soul to read them," said the Honourable John Ruffin in a very grave voice.

"Would it?" said the duke.

"It would. But I thought I would come down, in case she made a descent and you wanted some one to stand by and stiffen you."

"Do you know, I don't think I do," said the duke. "I really believe I can stick it out on my own."

"Good," said the Honourable John Ruffin.

"All the same I'm glad you came. If we get beyond having a tremendous row, we shall very likely want some one to arrange things for us," said the duke.

"I shouldn't think a tremendous row was quite your game," said the Honourable John Ruffin thoughtfully.

"Oh, *I'm* not going to row. But you know what Caroline is: she can have all the row there is to have, without any help from any one," said the duke. "I'm just going to sit tight as wax and let her wear herself out, if she does start rowing."

"That is undoubtedly the course for a man of sense to pursue," said the Honourable John Ruffin in a tone of approval.

The duke was on tenterhooks the next day, for though he was braced for the struggle with the duchess, he found the uncertainty when that struggle would begin trying. Then he was taking his afternoon tea with the Honourable John Ruffin on the cedar lawn; Ronald and Pollyooly mindful of the cakes, had sociably joined them; and they were laughing at a story the Honourable John Ruffin was telling them, when he stopped short, staring at the entrance to the lawn. They turned to see the duchess standing in it, and surveying them with the eyes of an avenging angel.

They all rose; and the Honourable John Ruffin said calmly:

"How are you, Caroline? I suppose you motored down. Charming weather for motoring."

"Very," said the duchess in a terrible voice. "And a charming gathering I find at the end of it."

"Yes; sit down and have some tea. You must be thirsty," said the Honourable John Ruffin.

"How are you, Caroline? Sit down and have some tea," said the duke, seizing on the opening, in rather uncertain tones.

"Tea!" said the duchess, in a yet more terrible voice.

"And bread and butter," said the duke hastily.

"Do you think I came here to drink *tea*?" said the duchess in the tone of one who had come to drink blood.

"A lemon squash then," said the duke hastily.

"I haven't come here to drink tea, or lemon squashes," said the duchess. "I've come to learn what this means—to put an end to this ridiculous farce?"

"Eh? What? What farce?" said the duke.

"This farcical substitution of this wicked child, Mary Bride, for Marion," said the duchess, glaring at Pollyooly.

"But you're not going to do any substituting. I won't have it," said the duke firmly.

"Me? It's you! You've done it already!" cried the duchess, with a sudden note of astonishment in her voice.

The duke shook his head, and with a smile of superior knowledge said firmly:

"It won't do, Caroline. It's no good your trying it on."

The duchess gasped: "What do you mean? What *do* you mean?" she cried; and her tone was now all astonishment.

The Honourable John Ruffin created a diversion by saying:

"As far as I can make out this is a private matter; and little pitchers have long ears. Come along, little pitchers." And he was sweeping Pollyooly and Ronald off the lawn.

The duchess glared at him, and stopped them for a moment with the words:

"Is this your doing, John?"

"Heavens, no! Osterley is the originator, and organiser, and perpetrator of the whole arrangement," he cried over his shoulder in a tone which carried conviction; and he vanished with the children.

The duchess turned and glared again at the duke, as if she could not believe her eyes; she looked almost as if she saw him for the first time.

"Sit down and have some tea. You must be wanting it," said the duke firmly; and he began to pour it out.

The duchess sat down, with a somewhat helpless air, still staring at him. Matters seemed to be going differently from what she had expected. Her fine brown eyes looked very big.

"You did this all yourself?" she said, in a somewhat breathless voice.

"Did what? Two lumps, isn't it?" said the duke, putting two lumps into the cup and handing it to her.

"Deliberately substituted a strange child for your own," said the duchess solemnly.

"Oh, that," said the duke carelessly. "That's all right. You needn't worry about that. I've quite taken to Mary Bride. She's so—so companionable—and—and as clever as they make 'em, and as pretty as a picture. She makes a ripping Lady Marion Ricksborough. Why, when she comes into a room, or on to a lawn, it's beginning to make as much sensation as if it were yourself. I was awfully lucky to get hold of her." His tone had grown truly enthusiastic.

The duchess ground her teeth and cried:

"And do you think I'm going to stand it?"

"Stand it? I thought you'd like it," said the duke in a perplexed tone. "Of course I'm not going to bother you about Marion any more; you can keep her. And it's all so deucedly comfortable; you've got the Marion you want, and I've got the Marion I want. And so we're both happy." And he smiled amiably.

"Happy! Happy when a strange child is usurping the place of my child?" cried the duchess furiously.

"Oh, that's all right. Marion's got *you*," said the duke. "Besides, I'm not going to go all my life without any family. It wouldn't be fair; and you've no right to expect it. I say, how jolly you're looking!"

"Jolly!" said the duchess thickly.

"Well, pretty then. And your figure is better than ever—perfectly ripping," said the duke with enthusiasm.

"You can leave me out of it!" cried the duchess in a tone of the last exasperation. "And if you think I'm going to stand this, I'm not!"

"But what are you going to do about it?" said the duke mildly.

"Stop it!" said the duchess through her set teeth.

"But you can't stop it," said the duke in his most amiable tone. "I'm getting domesticated, and I'm bent on having something in the way of a family. Set on it. Of course you can say that your Marion is Lady Marion Ricksborough; and I shall say that mine is. And some people will believe you, but most people will believe me. And of course I shall settle a good lump sum on Mary Bride when she marries, and leave her all the unentailed property."

"Oh, but it's impossible!" cried the duchess writhing in her chair. "Leaving your child out in the cold for a perfect stranger!"

"But she isn't. I tell you, she and I get on like a house on fire," said the duke with some impatience. "And it's perfectly all right; you stick to your Marion; and I'll stick to mine."

The duchess rose and cried:

"It's abominable! The most cold-blooded thing I ever heard of! And if you think you're going to get rid of us like this, you're wrong! I stay here till this matter has been put right."

"Oh, I don't want to get rid of *you*," said the duke amiably.

The duchess ground her teeth and walked across the lawn with the air of a Boadicea saving her country. The duke watched her graceful figure till it disappeared through a long window into the pink drawing-room, with admiring eyes. Then he smiled a Machiavellian smile.

The duchess went to her rooms in a mood of seething, but somewhat helpless, fury. She was softened a little by finding them just as she had left them two years before. Plainly some one had taken care of the clothes she had left behind her; and her anxiety about a dress to dine in was lulled to rest. She thought for a while that she would go and berate Pollyooly; but she came to the conclusion that it would be absurd to blame her for the action of the duke. It was much more annoying to find that she could not reasonably blame the duke. She was forced to admit that he had a right to the domestic life, if he wished for it. She was also annoyed to feel an uncommonly pleasant sense of home-coming. She resented it, but she could not rid herself of it.

She came to dinner very dignified and stern; but the Honourable John Ruffin saw to it that the meal was unconstrained. He spared no effort to keep the talk in a light vein; and the duke, after his talk with the duchess that afternoon, was sufficiently at his ease to second him to the best of his not very great ability. He won the Honourable John Ruffin's golden opinions by remembering the other two occasions on which the duchess had worn the gown she was wearing to-night.

Little by little, against her will, she thawed. The sense of home-coming grew stronger. The easy, reminiscent talk— reminiscent of pleasant days—the familiar room, and, perhaps, her favourite brand of champagne, softened her till her smiles came easily. Moreover it was delightful to be amused again; and it was borne suddenly in upon her that the months she had been living in hiding had been tiresome, boring months, from the point of view of life, utterly wasted months. Again and again she looked at the duke as if she saw him for the first time. Plainly she was amending her opinion of him.

She yielded readily to the entreaties of the two men to stop and drink her coffee and smoke her cigarette with them. The Honourable John Ruffin talked on; she laughed several times. Then, having finished his cigarette, and lighted a cigar, he said:

"I have a sonnet to write to the eyebrow of a lady—no, Caroline: you do not know her—and I must have perfect solitude, by the side of still water, in the moonlight. So I am going down to the long pool; and I must on no account be interrupted. So long."

And he went quickly through the long window.

He spoke quickly and went quickly, before the duchess could suggest that he should wait a while. She felt unequal to a tete-a-tete with her husband, and nervously she half rose.

"Oh, don't you rush away too," said the duke somewhat plaintively.

She sank back into her chair.

The duke looked at her for a while in silence with eyes full of an admiration at once gratifying and discomfiting; then he said:

"I say, Caroline, can you remember what it was we first quarrelled about?"

The duchess knitted her brow in the effort to recall it, and said:

"No, I can't. Oh, yes! You grumbled at the way my hair was done." Then she added in a tone of triumph, "And I've done it exactly the same ever since; it's done like it now!"

"Something must have upset me, for it looks perfectly ripping," said the duke with warm conviction.

The duchess felt herself blushing under his admiring eyes, and disliked herself very much for doing so.

She rose hastily and said:

"I think I'll go into the garden."

This time the duke let her go. He finished his cigar before he followed her. He found her walking up and down the cedar lawn; and when the moonlight fell on her face, he saw that it was troubled.

He fell into step beside her and said with enthusiasm:

Edgar Jepson

"It's a ripping night."

She said nothing; and they crossed the lawn and turned.

He said, again with enthusiasm:

"I do like this lawn. I first kissed you under that old tree."

The duchess started to leave the lawn with some speed.

The duke kept pace with her.

Half-way across the lawn he said in an affectionate tone:

"There's no need for you to fret about Marion, old girl. You can arrange it just as you like."

Then deftly, he slipped his arm round her waist.

"How dare you, Archie?" she cried, and made to thrust him away with some vigour.

It was not enough vigour. The duke's arm did not slip; indeed he tightened his clasp as he said:

"I could do much better with a complete family—a wife and a daughter."

"After the way you've behaved!" cried the duchess.

"Oh, well, one doesn't always behave the same. One changes," said the duke.

Three days later Pollyooly and Ronald stood by a gate at the end of the home wood, awaiting the coming of the motor car, in which the Honourable John Ruffin was bringing the real

Lady Marion Ricksborough to slip quietly into the place which Pollyooly had occupied with such signal success. The Lump, in the care of Emily Gibbs, was already speeding in the train to London, to be met at Waterloo and conveyed to the Temple by Mrs. Brown.

Ronald looked gloomy; and an air of sadness marred Pollyooly's serenity.

"It's perfectly rotten your going off like this—before we've done half the things we were going to. Why on earth couldn't uncle have waited till the end of the holidays to make the change?" said Ronald in a bitterly aggrieved tone.

"Well, you'll have Marion to go about with you," said Pollyooly.

"Nothing doing!" snapped Ronald.

His vehemence pleased her.

"It's a pity," she said sadly. "It's been splendid; and I'm awfully sorry to have to go."

Then her face cleared and brightened into an angel smile; she crinkled in her pocket the five ten-pound notes which the grateful duke had given her; and added:

"But it's splendid to think that with what I've got in the Savings Bank and this, I can keep the Lump out of the workhouse for years and years!"

Edgar Jepson

Choose from Thousands of 1stWorldLibrary Classics By

A. M. Barnard
Ada Leverson
Adolphus William Ward
Aesop
Agatha Christie
Alexander Aaronsohn
Alexander Kielland
Alexandre Dumas
Alfred Gatty
Alfred Ollivant
Alice Duer Miller
Alice Turner Curtis
Alice Dunbar
Allen Chapman
Alleyne Ireland
Ambrose Bierce
Amelia E. Barr
Amory H. Bradford
Andrew Lang
Andrew McFarland Davis
Andy Adams
Angela Brazil
Anna Alice Chapin
Anna Sewell
Annie Besant
Annie Hamilton Donnell
Annie Payson Call
Annie Roe Carr
Annonaymous
Anton Chekhov
Archibald Lee Fletcher
Arnold Bennett
Arthur C. Benson
Arthur Conan Doyle
Arthur M. Winfield
Arthur Ransome
Arthur Schnitzler
Arthur Train
Atticus
B.H. Baden-Powell
B. M. Bower
B. C. Chatterjee
Baroness Emmuska Orczy
Baroness Orczy
Basil King
Bayard Taylor
Ben Macomber
Bertha Muzzy Bower
Bjornstjerne Bjornson

Booth Tarkington
Boyd Cable
Bram Stoker
C. Collodi
C. E. Orr
C. M. Ingleby
Carolyn Wells
Catherine Parr Traill
Charles A. Eastman
Charles Amory Beach
Charles Dickens
Charles Dudley Warner
Charles Farrar Browne
Charles Ives
Charles Kingsley
Charles Klein
Charles Hanson Towne
Charles Lathrop Pack
Charles Romyn Dake
Charles Whibley
Charles Willing Beale
Charlotte M. Braeme
Charlotte M. Yonge
Charlotte Perkins Stetson
Clair W. Hayes
Clarence Day Jr.
Clarence E. Mulford
Clemence Housman
Confucius
Coningsby Dawson
Cornelis DeWitt Wilcox
Cyril Burleigh
D. H. Lawrence
Daniel Defoe
David Garnett
Dinah Craik
Don Carlos Janes
Donald Keyhoe
Dorothy Kilner
Dougan Clark
Douglas Fairbanks
E. Nesbit
E. P. Roe
E. Phillips Oppenheim
E. S. Brooks
Earl Barnes
Edgar Rice Burroughs
Edith Van Dyne
Edith Wharton

Edward Everett Hale
Edward J. O'Biren
Edward S. Ellis
Edwin L. Arnold
Eleanor Atkins
Eleanor Hallowell Abbott
Eliot Gregory
Elizabeth Gaskell
Elizabeth McCracken
Elizabeth Von Arnim
Ellem Key
Emerson Hough
Emilie F. Carlen
Emily Bronte
Emily Dickinson
Enid Bagnold
Enilor Macartney Lane
Erasmus W. Jones
Ernie Howard Pie
Ethel May Dell
Ethel Turner
Ethel Watts Mumford
Eugene Sue
Eugenie Foa
Eugene Wood
Eustace Hale Ball
Evelyn Everett-green
Everard Cotes
F. H. Cheley
F. J. Cross
F. Marion Crawford
Fannie E. Newberry
Federick Austin Ogg
Ferdinand Ossendowski
Fergus Hume
Florence A. Kilpatrick
Fremont B. Deering
Francis Bacon
Francis Darwin
Frances Hodgson Burnett
Frances Parkinson Keyes
Frank Gee Patchin
Frank Harris
Frank Jewett Mather
Frank L. Packard
Frank V. Webster
Frederic Stewart Isham
Frederick Trevor Hill
Frederick Winslow Taylor

Friedrich Kerst
Friedrich Nietzsche
Fyodor Dostoyevsky
G.A. Henty
G.K. Chesterton
Gabrielle E. Jackson
Garrett P. Serviss
Gaston Leroux
George A. Warren
George Ade
Geroge Bernard Shaw
George Cary Eggleston
George Durston
George Ebers
George Eliot
George Gissing
George MacDonald
George Meredith
George Orwell
George Sylvester Viereck
George Tucker
George W. Cable
George Wharton James
Gertrude Atherton
Gordon Casserly
Grace E. King
Grace Gallatin
Grace Greenwood
Grant Allen
Guillermo A. Sherwell
Gulielma Zollinger
Gustav Flaubert
H. A. Cody
H. B. Irving
H.C. Bailey
H. G. Wells
H. H. Munro
H. Irving Hancock
H. R. Naylor
H. Rider Haggard
H. W. C. Davis
Haldeman Julius
Hall Caine
Hamilton Wright Mabie
Hans Christian Andersen
Harold Avery
Harold McGrath
Harriet Beecher Stowe
Harry Castlemon
Harry Coghill
Harry Houidini

Hayden Carruth
Helent Hunt Jackson
Helen Nicolay
Hendrik Conscience
Hendy David Thoreau
Henri Barbusse
Henrik Ibsen
Henry Adams
Henry Ford
Henry Frost
Henry James
Henry Jones Ford
Henry Seton Merriman
Henry W Longfellow
Herbert A. Giles
Herbert Carter
Herbert N. Casson
Herman Hesse
Hildegard G. Frey
Homer
Honore De Balzac
Horace B. Day
Horace Walpole
Horatio Alger Jr.
Howard Pyle
Howard R. Garis
Hugh Lofting
Hugh Walpole
Humphry Ward
Ian Maclaren
Inez Haynes Gillmore
Irving Bacheller
Isabel Cecilia Williams
Isabel Hornibrook
Israel Abrahams
Ivan Turgenev
J.G.Austin
J. Henri Fabre
J. M. Barrie
J. M. Walsh
J. Macdonald Oxley
J. R. Miller
J. S. Fletcher
J. S. Knowles
J. Storer Clouston
J. W. Duffield
Jack London
Jacob Abbott
James Allen
James Andrews
James Baldwin

James Branch Cabell
James DeMille
James Joyce
James Lane Allen
James Lane Allen
James Oliver Curwood
James Oppenheim
James Otis
James R. Driscoll
Jane Abbott
Jane Austen
Jane L. Stewart
Janet Aldridge
Jens Peter Jacobsen
Jerome K. Jerome
Jessie Graham Flower
John Buchan
John Burroughs
John Cournos
John F. Kennedy
John Gay
John Glasworthy
John Habberton
John Joy Bell
John Kendrick Bangs
John Milton
John Philip Sousa
John Taintor Foote
Jonas Lauritz Idemil Lie
Jonathan Swift
Joseph A. Altsheler
Joseph Carey
Joseph Conrad
Joseph E. Badger Jr
Joseph Hergesheimer
Joseph Jacobs
Jules Vernes
Julian Hawthrone
Julie A Lippmann
Justin Huntly McCarthy
Kakuzo Okakura
Karle Wilson Baker
Kate Chopin
Kenneth Grahame
Kenneth McGaffey
Kate Langley Bosher
Kate Langley Bosher
Katherine Cecil Thurston
Katherine Stokes
L. A. Abbot
L. T. Meade

L. Frank Baum
Latta Griswold
Laura Dent Crane
Laura Lee Hope
Laurence Housman
Lawrence Beasley
Leo Tolstoy
Leonid Andreyev
Lewis Carroll
Lewis Sperry Chafer
Lilian Bell
Lloyd Osbourne
Louis Hughes
Louis Joseph Vance
Louis Tracy
Louisa May Alcott
Lucy Fitch Perkins
Lucy Maud Montgomery
Luther Benson
Lydia Miller Middleton
Lyndon Orr
M. Corvus
M. H. Adams
Margaret E. Sangster
Margret Howth
Margaret Vandercook
Margaret W. Hungerford
Margret Penrose
Maria Edgeworth
Maria Thompson Daviess
Mariano Azuela
Marion Polk Angellotti
Mark Overton
Mark Twain
Mary Austin
Mary Catherine Crowley
Mary Cole
Mary Hastings Bradley
Mary Roberts Rinehart
Mary Rowlandson
M. Wollstonecraft Shelley
Maud Lindsay
Max Beerbohm
Myra Kelly
Nathaniel Hawthrone
Nicolo Machiavelli
O. F. Walton
Oscar Wilde

Owen Johnson
P.G. Wodehouse
Paul and Mabel Thorne
Paul G. Tomlinson
Paul Severing
Percy Brebner
Percy Keese Fitzhugh
Peter B. Kyne
Plato
Quincy Allen
R. Derby Holmes
R. L. Stevenson
R. S. Ball
Rabindranath Tagore
Rahul Alvares
Ralph Bonehill
Ralph Henry Barbour
Ralph Victor
Ralph Waldo Emmerson
Rene Descartes
Ray Cummings
Rex Beach
Rex E. Beach
Richard Harding Davis
Richard Jefferies
Richard Le Gallienne
Robert Barr
Robert Frost
Robert Gordon Anderson
Robert L. Drake
Robert Lansing
Robert Lynd
Robert Michael Ballantyne
Robert W. Chambers
Rosa Nouchette Carey
Rudyard Kipling
Saint Augustine
Samuel B. Allison
Samuel Hopkins Adams
Sarah Bernhardt
Sarah C. Hallowell
Selma Lagerlof
Sherwood Anderson
Sigmund Freud
Standish O'Grady
Stanley Weyman
Stella Benson
Stella M. Francis

Stephen Crane
Stewart Edward White
Stijn Streuvels
Swami Abhedananda
Swami Parmananda
T. S. Ackland
T. S. Arthur
The Princess Der Ling
Thomas A. Janvier
Thomas A Kempis
Thomas Anderton
Thomas Bailey Aldrich
Thomas Bulfinch
Thomas De Quincey
Thomas Dixon
Thomas H. Huxley
Thomas Hardy
Thomas More
Thornton W. Burgess
U. S. Grant
Upton Sinclair
Valentine Williams
Various Authors
Vaughan Kester
Victor Appleton
Victor G. Durham
Victoria Cross
Virginia Woolf
Wadsworth Camp
Walter Camp
Walter Scott
Washington Irving
Wilbur Lawton
Wilkie Collins
Willa Cather
Willard F. Baker
William Dean Howells
William le Queux
W. Makepeace Thackeray
William W. Walter
William Shakespeare
Winston Churchill
Yei Theodora Ozaki
Yogi Ramacharaka
Young E. Allison
Zane Grey